Dvořák

Neil Butterworth.

Jendo,

I hope music will always be a big part of your life .... whether for "peace", "inner peace", a sense of "tranquility" or "togetherness within yourself".....with all my heart, Susan

CHRISTMAS 1987

The Illustrated Lives of the Great Composers.

Dvořák

Neil Butterworth.

Omnibus Press
London/New York/Sydney/Cologne

Cover design and art direction by Pearce Marchbank.
Cover photography by George Taylor, Rembrandt Bros.
Cover styled by Annie Hanson.
Properties by The Lacquer Chest, Edward Withers, Ken Paul.

Printed and bound in Hungary.

Order No. OP 42423
UK ISBN 0.7119.0256.9
US ISBN 0.89524.206.0

Exclusive Distributors:
Book Sales Limited,
78 Newman Street,
London W1P 3LA,
England.
Omnibus Press,
GPO Box 3304,
Sydney,
NSW 2001,
Australia.
Cherry Lane Books,
PO Box 430,
Port Chester,
N.Y. 10573,
U.S.A.
To The Music Trade Only:
Music Sales Limited,
78 Newman Street,
London W1P 3LA,
England.

Contents

7

Acknowledgements

I am very grateful for the help received in the completion of this book from Mozelle Moshansky and Nigel Simeone. Mozelle Moshansky undertook the task of preparing my manuscript for publication, while to Nigel Simeone I am indebted for permission to make use of photographs and music examples drawn from his extensive private collection. Thanks for their support must go also to Ian Morley-Clarke and Robert Hardcastle at Midas Books.

Chapter 1

The Background

'Long live the truth! Long live our rights! Long live the protectors of our glorious homeland!'—Karel Sabina

The history of Bohemia is a long and colourful one. During the 6th Century, Slavic peoples for the first time settled in what is today Czechoslovakia. Some three centuries hence, a Moravian Empire was formed by the Slav Czechs of Moravia and Bohemia and the Slovaks of Slovakia: a fledgling nation that soon found itself in danger from the Magyars, an obstreperous and war-like people who occupied the Danube basin and were ideally placed to drive a wedge between the Eastern and Western Slavs.

Indeed, after the death in 929 of Prince Václav, the establishment of a Polish state in the North by Slav tribes from the Vistula and Oder regions quickly brought about the downfall of the new Empire. Bohemia and Moravia, however, managed to retain their unity for a further two hundred years under Prěmyslid dynasty.*

So successful was this union that even the widespread devastation caused by an invasion of Tartars from Russia in 1241, could not restrain Bohemia from reaching in the middle of the 13th Century the height of its power, with borders stretching far and wide, from the Adriatic to the Oder. However on the death of Prěmysl II in 1278, much of the realm was lost to Austria, and in 1310 the rule of Bohemia passed to the House of Luxembourg under King John.

* The best-known victim of this turbulent period is probably Good King Wenceslas, murdered in the 10th century by Boleslav the Wicked.

The hymn *Lord Have Mercy Upon Us* certainly dates back to the 13th century. This is the earliest known manuscript which is itself dated 1397.

The succession of John's son Charles IV, in 1346, led to what has been called Bohemia's 'Golden Age'. As the country emerged from the Middle Ages into the Renaissance, Czech painting, sculpture, architecture and literature all flourished. The first of its kind in Central Europe, Charles University in Prague was founded in 1348.

Economic prosperity also accelerated. At one time the silver mines of Kutná Hora were supplying coinage for the whole of Europe.

Husinec, birthplace of the great religious reformer John Hus.

Charles IV was also Emperor of Germany and, effectively the founder of the Austro-Hungarian Empire. Only after the death of his successor, Václav, did Bohemia's eminent position begin to decline as religious discord spread.

Jan Hus (c. 1373-1415) is today remembered not only as a religious reformer but also as a great patriotic leader. Born in Prague and educated at the Charles University, Hus became Professor of Philology and, in 1402, Rector of the latter. Like John Wycliffe, whom he greatly admired, he rejected the authority of the Pope, preaching vehemently against ecclesiastical abuses. His national pride led him to write in Czech as well as Latin, and he composed a number of popular hymns in his own language.

Not surprisingly, Hus soon found himself excommunicated, and in 1413 summoned before the Council of Constance. After a trial he was, on 6 July 1415, burnt at the stake. Enraged, his followers 'The Hussites' could not be dealt with so easily, becoming a nationalist party opposed implacably to both the Germans and the Vatican.

3

Manuscript of the old Hussite hymn *Ye Warriors of God*, from the Jistebnice Hymnal.

In 1526 the crown of Bohemia passed to Archduke Ferdinand I of Austria, brother to Charles V, the Hapsburg Holy Roman Emperor. The opposition to Catholicism, though, continued. In 1618, the Czech nobles, under the Calvinist King Ferdinand V, rose against the Austrian domination, but only two years later were defeated by the forces of the Emperor Ferdinand II at the Battle of the White Mountain on the outskirts of Prague. Thereafter, the people were forced to become Catholics, German was declared the official language and Czech culture was suppressed. During the Thirty Years' War that followed, the population of Bohemia was reduced from 3 million to about 900,000, and three centuries were to pass before the Czech people regained their independence from Austria.

Dvořák was eventually to pay his own tribute to Hus with the overture *Husitská (The Hussites),* the first part of an intended but uncompleted trilogy. Composed in 1883, it makes use of two Hussite hymns, *Ye Warriors of God* and the *St. Wenceslas Chorale.* It is interesting to note that Smetana, the father of modern Bohemian

4

music, had already made use of the first of these hymns in both *Tábor* (1878) and *Blaník* (1879), symphonic poems that form part of the cycle *Má Vlast*. They were first performed in the year before Dvořák wrote his overture. A much later Czech composer, Karel Husa (b. 1921) has incorporated, as a symbol of resistance during a more recent crisis in the troubled history of Czechoslovakia, the same hymn into his *Music for Prague 1968*.

It is interesting also to record that the Battle of the White Mountain is commemorated in Dvořák's first choral work *The Heirs of the White Mountain*, a setting for chorus and orchestra of a poem by Vítězslav Hálek completed in 1872.

On his European travels in 1772, Dr. Burney noted that the Bohemians were the most musical people of Germany, perhaps even of Europe. He was much impressed at seeing young children in schools being taught to sing and to play musical instruments.

The town of Tábor, one of the strongholds of the Hussite brethren.

Jiří Benda

Leopold Koželuh

Even in the 17th Century, Bohemian composers were gaining international reputations. Heinrich Biber (1644-1704), wrote a set of fifteen Mystery 'Rosary' Sonatas for violin and continuo, based on Catholic devotions, which became widely known.

For so small a country, Bohemia gave birth in the 18th Century to a remarkable number of talented composers. Although a few, such as František Mica (1694-1744), František Xaver Brixi (1732-1771) and Jan Jakub Ryba (1765-1815) were content to stay at home, many others travelled across the Continent, seeking out posts at the most important courts and churches, more especially those of Italy and Germany.

Anton Rejcha

Fr. Krommer

6

V. J. Tomášek   Fr. Škroup

Christoph Willibald Gluck was born near Prague in 1714, but soon moved away, first to Vienna and later to Paris, where he acquired great fame as an opera composer.

Others, in order to conceal their rather rustic origins, changed their names; Franz Anton Rössler (1746-1792), the composer of many symphonies and concertos, preferred to be known as Francesco Antonio Rosetti. The Moravian František Kramář (1759-1831), wrote a great deal of music for wind instruments, became Franz Krommer. Until quite recently he was referred to somewhat confusingly as Krommer-Kramar!

The notable Benda family of Altbenatsky produced as many composers as the Bach family in Germany. František (Franz) (1709-1786), Jan (Johann) (1713-1752), Jiří (Georg) 1722-1795), Joseph (1724-1804), Friedrich Wilhelm (1745-1814), Friedrich Ludwig (1752-1792) and Karl (1748-1836) all held posts in Germany.

The court of Mannheim received a steady flow of Bohemians including Franz Xavier Richter (1709-1789), Jan Václav (Johann) Stamic (or Stamitz) (1717-1757), his son Karl Philipp (1745-1801) and Antonín Fils (1730-1760).

To Italy went Bohuslav Černohrský (1684-1742), the composer of organ music, and two others who devoted themselves principally to opera: Florian Gassman

(1729-1774) and Josef Mysliveček (1737-1781), the latter being visited in Milan by Mozart in 1770.

Another important Bohemian musician was Antonín Rejcha (1770-1836), an exact contemporary and friend of Beethoven and a fellow member of the Bonn orchestra. After a few years in Vienna he settled in Paris. The much-travelled Jan Ladislav Dušík (Johann Dussek) as a young man left his native Bohemia and wandered the length and breadth of Germany, Holland, Russia, France and England where he was much respected as a pianist.

Johann Wenzel Tomášchek (1774-1850), a noted composer of piano music, preferred to remain in Bohemia and died in Prague after a distinguished career as a teacher. His pupil Jan Václav Hugo Voříšek was born in Eastern Bohemia in 1791. After study in Prague with Tomášchek, he however chose to move in 1813 to Vienna, becoming a pupil of Hummel and Moscheles. Voříšek's Symphony in D shows a remarkable original talent, but the composer died of tuberculosis in 1825 at the age of thirty-three.

The very first Czech opera, *The Tinker*, was produced with great success in 1826, at the State Opera in Prague. The composer, today largely forgotten, was František Škroup (1801-1862), trained as a lawyer, but soon appointed conductor at the State Opera, in 1827 the first Czech to hold the post. Škroup also composed the Czech national anthem *Kde domov můj?*, which Dvořák in 1882 incorporated into his overture *My Home*.

Chapter 2

Early Years

'A child of nature, who did not stop to think and said on paper anything which came into his mind'—Stanford

Antonín Leopold Dvořák was born at the tiny Bohemian village of Nelahozeves about eighteen miles north of Prague on the river Vitara, on 8 September 1841. A sleepy little place, Nelahozeves was set in low hills and surrounded by countryside, and was dominated by the huge square castle which had been in the possession of the Lobkowitz family since 1623. Prince Franz Joseph Max Lobkowitz (1772-1816) was a friend and important patron of the young Beethoven.

Antonín was the eldest of nine children, eight of whom survived childhood. His father, František (an accomplished amateur musician who played the violin and zither and composed dance tunes) had followed his own father in business as an inn-keeper and butcher. On 17 November 1840 he had married Anna Zdeňková, a servant in the household of Prince Lobkowitz and daughter of one of the Prince's stewards.

Antonín grew up amidst the simple life of a country community. His deep religious adherence to the Catholic Church, instilled at a very early age, lasted the whole of his life. As a boy he was surrounded additionally by the folk songs and dances of the Bohemian people.

From Josef Spitz, the village schoolmaster and organist, he learnt to play the violin and the boy was soon performing beside his father in instrumental ensembles at weddings and other celebrations.

Like all the village children, he was taught in school

Dvořák's birthplace was Nelahozeves, a small village in Bohemia, about 18 miles north of Prague *(from an engraving c.1840)*.

to read music and he also sang in the church choir. By the time he left school shortly before his twelfth birthday in 1853, he had received a valuable basic training in all aspects of music.*

The following year, his mother's younger brother Zdeněk, who had no children of his own, offered to help the family by looking after Antonín at Zlonice, a town some twenty miles from Nelahozeves. Here he was apprenticed as a butcher, but at the same time was able to continue musical studies with another schoolmaster organist, Antonín Liehmann (1808-1879). Liehmann, a versatile if short-tempered musician, played several instruments and composed much music for the local orchestra which he conducted.

The young Dvořák received lessons in organ, piano and viola and was soon taking his place in the orchestra. Many years later he wrote of his teacher:

* Comparatively little is known of Dvořák's schooling. The schoolhouse was eventually burnt down, and with it all the school records.

Liehmann was a good musician, but he was quick tempered and still taught according to the old methods; if a pupil could not play a passage, he got as many cuffs as there were notes on the sheet. He could also read and play figured bass fluently, and taught us to do the same.

On the advice of Uncle Zdeněk, the Dvořák family in 1855 moved to Zlonice where František soon found himself managing *The Big Inn*. In November 1856, the fifteen-year-old Antonín successfully completed his apprenticeship as a butcher, and was awarded his certificate of proficiency:

We, the undersigned office-holders of the honourable Town Guild of Butchers in Zlonice, do by these present bear witness and confirm that Antoníus Dvořák of Nelahozeves, born on the 8th September 1841, of Roman Catholic denomination, was bound as an apprentice in the year 1854, on the fifth of the month of November, at the opening of the

Nelahozeves Castle as it stands today.

Dvořák's family home.

The entry in the Nelahozeves registry showing the birth of Antonín Dvořák in 1841.

Guild Fund, to the butcher's trade, the apprenticeship to run from the 1st November for two years. In as far as the aforesaid Antonius Dvořák conducted himself during the specified period of two years of his apprenticeship honestly, faithfully and industriously, and having learned, as is testified to by his Master, Jan Roubal, the trade of butcher well and properly, he was presented on the self-same 1st November, 1856 to the assembled gathering under the Chairmanship of the P.T. superintendant of this Guild and declared in due order to have served his apprenticeship.

Dvořák's father, František Dvořák (1814-1894) and his aunt Josefina Dušková with whom he stayed when he first went to Prague.

The room in which Dvořák was born.

Having made out for the above-named Antonius Dvořák this CERTIFICATE OF APPRENTICESHIP entitling him to carry on the trade of butcher, we beg that he should be recognised as a properly taught butcher's journeyman and everywhere received with courtesy. In witness whereof this certificate of apprenticeship is awarded by the undersigned and under the Great Seal Ordinary.

In order to improve his German Antonín was then sent to Česká Kamenice on the border with Saxony. Anyone in Bohemia who wished to make something of himself—even as an inn-keeper—had to be fluent in German. Dvořák it seems was acutely aware of his shortcomings in this respect when he became a student in Prague. At the same time, he continued his musical studies in harmony and organ, and he once again sang in the church choir.

When he returned to Zlonice in the following year, he found the Dvořák family business waning rather than waxing, and in financial difficulties. Once again Uncle Zdeněk came to the rescue. If Antonín was another mouth to be fed, the sooner he could make his own way, the better. Zdeněk consequently persuaded

Dvořák received his early education at the local village school in Nelahozeves.

Karel Fr. Pietsch, Director of the Organ School at Prague was succeeded on his death in 1858 by Josef Krejčí.

his brother-in-law to allow his son to devote himself to music, himself offering to pay for Antonín to study at the Organ School in Prague.

The Institute for Church Music (the 'Organ School' in Prague) was founded in 1830 and based exclusively on traditional German practices. When Antonín was accepted there in August 1857, the director was Karel F. Pietsch (1789-1858). A year later, he was succeeded by Josef Krejčí (1822-1881).

Teaching was on conservative lines, unsympathetic to current trends. Dvořák spoke little of his experience at this time but his pupil Josef Michl recounts the composer's remarks to the effect that:

At the organ school everything smelt of mould, even the organ. Anybody who wanted to learn anything had to know German. Anyone who knew German could be dux of the class, but if he did not know German, he could not. My knowledge of German was poor, and even if I knew something, I could not get it out. My fellow students looked a little down their noses at me and laughed at me behind my back.

A report on Dvořák from the School makes interesting reading:

(He possesses) an excellent but more practical talent. Practical knowledge and accomplishment seem to be his aim. In theory he is somewhat weaker.

14

Dvořák's organ teacher was Josef Foerster (1833-1907), father of the composer Josef Bohuslav Foerster (1859-1951). He received, however, no composition lessons as such and remained always self-taught in this respect. As he said, 'I study with the birds, flowers, God and myself'.

For his first year in Prague, this rather gauche youngster 'up from the country' stayed in the house of his cousin, Marie Plívová, whose daughter Anna was to leave revealing reminiscences of their student lodger.

Dvořák studied at the Organ School from 1857 to 1859.

When the Plívé household became too crowded, Dvořák moved in with his uncle Václav Dušek. About the same time, his Uncle Zdeněk in Zlonice became unable to continue financial support for his nephew's studies, and Dvořák was compelled for a time to fend for himself as best he could by teaching and playing the viola.

In 1853, Dvořák's family had moved to Zlonice.

Musical activities outside the Organ School probably proved of more lasting benefit to him than the actual tuition he was receiving. As a member of the orchestra of the Society of St. Cecilia he gained, under the conductorship of Antonín Apt, valuable practical experience. It was from this direct contact that Dvořák was, like Elgar, to acquire his masterly knowledge of the orchestra.

'The Great Inn', Zlonice, which Dvořák's father rented in 1854.

Josef Foerster, organist and teacher of church music at the Prague Organ School.

On leaving the Organ School in 1859, Dvořák joined Karel Komzák's Band as a viola player. Komzák, later to become a regimental bandmaster in the Austrian army, was the composer of popular music who was organist at the Prague Institute for Mental Cases where Dvořák sometimes played for him (it will be remembered that Elgar as a young man also played in a band at a lunatic asylum). The Band also performed in high-class cafés and included in their repertoire certain of the *Hungarian Dances* by Brahms, Dvořák's first acquaintance with that composer's music.

In November 1862, the Provisional Theatre was established in Prague for the production of Czech plays and operas. The Komzák Band became the nucleus of the orchestra there, playing two or three times a week.

On 8 February 1863, Dvořák played in the orchestra at a concert of music by Wagner, conducted by the composer. The experience made a deep impression upon him and for a while the shadow of Wagner lay heavily over the music he wrote.

Indeed, after leaving the Organ School, Dvořák had devoted an increasing amount of time to composition. Knowledge of this was, however, concealed even from his friends. Except for a few piano pieces, most of these

16

Young Dvořák received a great deal of encouragement from the choir-master at Zlonice, Josef Toman, and the local organist Antonin Liehmann, who also led the village band.

early works were destroyed. The earliest known compositions to survive are a String Quintet in A, dated 6 June 1861 and originally the composer's Opus 1, and—from March 1862—a Quartet in the same key.

In 1864, Dvořák was, for the third and final time, rejected for military service. During the same year, he fell in love with Josefina Čermáková, the sixteen-year-old daughter of a Prague goldsmith. For Josefina he composed a song cycle, *Cypresses,* but his attentions seem not to have impressed her. Four of these songs he published in 1882 as Opus 2; a further twelve of them he transcribed for string quartet.

1865 was to be a year of more compositional activity. The First Symphony, originally Opus 3, has the subtitle *The Bells of Zlonice,* and in the opening sections of the first and last movements, Dvořák does indeed produce in the orchestra bell-like sonorities as accompaniment to the principal themes. No doubt these effects evoked in the composer happy memories of his childhood.

Dvořák came to Prague in 1857 and lived there most of his life.

The Čermák sisters. Josefa was Dvořák's first love, but it was Anna (*seated at the piano*) he eventually married.

The originality of this work and of the Symphony in B flat, composed later in the same year has been overlooked by most writers. Yet it is difficult to find as early as this in most other symphonic composers—least of all those whose works the young Dvořák would have known—a similar expansive lyricism. Smetana's *Festive* Symphony of 1854 may have served as a model but the language is quite different. The symphonies of Brahms and Bruckner had yet to be written, and although Borodin was at work on his First Symphony, the bulk of the Russian symphonic output comes towards the end of the century. Traces of Wagner's influences may be heard in places in these early symphonies, but the design and idiom look forward to the mature Dvořák.

The Bells of Zlonice was composed with Dvořák's customary speed in February and March 1865 and submitted promptly to a competition in Germany. The score, however, appears not to have been returned and remained lost until 1923, the first performance following in 1936 in Brno. The composer himself by all accounts quite forgot about it, in later years omitting it from his own list of early works. Some of the thematic material, though, he did use in the *Silhouettes* for piano, completed some fourteen years after the symphony in 1879.

The Second Symphony occupied Dvořák between August and October 1865. The composer was evidently displeased with the result and it was only through the good offices of his friend Mořic Anger that the score was preserved. The première, under Adolf Čech, consequently did not take place until March 1888, by which time Dvořák had completed five other symphonies.

Also dating from 1865 is a Cello Concerto in A that remained unscored and unperformed. Many other pieces were destroyed by the composer including works for orchestra, a Clarinet Quintet and at least one setting of the Mass. Referring to discarded manuscripts, Dvořák once remarked laconically, 'I always have enough paper to make a fire'.

The Old Town Square: Prague *(from an engraving by V. Morstadt)*.

Chapter 3

Smetana and Opera

'Smetana has put on the stage a slice of real life, realistically seen'—František Bartoš.

In January 1866, at Prague's Provisional Theatre, Bedrich Smetana conducted the first performance of his opera *The Brandenburgers in Bohemia*. Its strongly nationalistic character made the production an instant success.

Smetana was duly appointed conductor at the Theatre, and later the same year directed the première of the comic opera *The Bartered Bride*. This firmly established Smetana's reputation in Prague and made a deep impression on Dvořák, who had played in the orchestra for both operas.

The Bartered Bride introduced a new kind of operatic form, having more in common in its use of ensembles with Mozart's stage works than with other contemporary operas. Like Mozart, Smetana was able to create real people, recognised easily by the audience as a reflection of their own lives and times. The twists and turns of the plot of *The Bartered Bride*, with its various intrigues and misunderstandings, remind one of Da Ponte's skilful manipulation of events and characters in his libretti for *The Marriage of Figaro* and *Cosi Fan Tutte*.

Although the public would have preferred another comedy, Smetana for his next opera, *Dalibor*, turned to a tragic historical subject. Based on an old legend, the plot could be interpreted in contemporary terms of the struggle of the Czech people.

The première of *Dalibor*, on 16th May 1868, also marked the laying of the foundation stone of the

Portrait of Dvořák
c. 1865.

21

By the time Dvořák arrived in Prague Bedřich Smetana (1824-1884) was the undisputed leader of Czech musical life. The portrait *(left)* dates from about 1861, the year in which the composer scored an immense success with his opera *The Bartered Bride*. Illustrated below is a scene from the 1956 Sadlers Wells production of this most famous of all Czech operas.

Prague National Theatre. Although the audience was enthusiastic, the critics unanimously condemned the work, more personal and less immediately tuneful than Smetana's previous works for the stage, for being insufficiently Czech in character and lacking the folk-song element of *The Bartered Bride*. The chromatic harmony, owing clearly much to Wagner and Liszt, was evidently not to the taste of Prague musicians. After only five performances, *Dalibor* was taken out of the repertoire.

During these formative years for Czech music, Dvořák had played in all Smetana's operas, and in the revivals of works by Škroup and other earlier Czech composers. With this practical experience of the opera house, and under the powerful dual influence of Smetana and Wagner, it was inevitable that he should consider writing for the stage sooner or later.

For his first attempt, Dvořák chose eventually a libretto on a historical subject—the wars between the Saxons and the Danes—by the German poet Karl Theodor Körner. As with *Dalibor*, the story could be

Programme of the first performance of the opera *Alfred* given in Olomouc in 1938.

Opposite

A portrait of the composer in his mid-twenties.

seen as a reflection of the Czech desire for independence from Austria.

Alfred was composed between May and October 1870, but the composer, aware of its weaknesses—the heroic story and the dances imitate Smetana, the orchestral writing is Wagnerian, and operatic conventions are incorporated awkwardly into the plot—made no attempt to gain a performance.

His second opera *The King and the Collier* was written between April and December 1871. The libretto,

24

adapted from a puppet play and set earlier by František Škroup, was this time exclusively Czech. Again, however, the shadows of Smetana and Wagner lay heavily on the music. For four weeks in the autumn of 1873, the Provisional Theatre rehearsed the opera, but problems for the singers made a production impossible and Dvořák withdrew it.*

In April 1874, Dvořák then took the unprecedented step of using the same libretto to compose a completely different setting of the opera, retaining not a single note of the original music. This second, simplified version turns away from Wagner to a more appropriate folk-song style for the subject of the story.

The Provisional Theatre, Prague, built in 1862.

* The Overture had been performed in April, 1872 under the direction of Smetana.

Dvořák played the viola in the Provisional Theatre Orchestra from 1862 to 1873. During the latter five years, the conductor was Smetána, and many of Dvořák's later creative were inspired by this period.

The plot is slight: a king out hunting loses his way and calls at the home of a poor charcoal-burner. The daughter of the house falls in love with the stranger and arouses the jealousy of her betrothed. The king reveals who he is and invites them all to his castle.

This version of the opera was produced at the Provisional Theatre on 24 November, 1874. Further revisions were made in the libretto and the music of the last act in 1887.

Chapter 4

Marriage

'She provided just the qualities Dvořák lacked, being energetic and practical in the affairs of daily life'—Alec Robertson, *Dvořák*

In 1870, the year he wrote *Alfred,* Dvořák also completed three String Quartets, those in B flat, D major and E minor, all performed privately with friends, but not published.

His first major public success came on 9 March 1873, in the New Town Theatre, Prague, with the première of his patriotic cantata for chorus and orchestra *The Heirs of the White Mountain.* The text, as we have seen, is a poem by Vitězslav Hálek commemorating the battle of the Czechs against the Austrians in 1620.

The Prague Hlahol Choir, which had at one time been conducted by Smetana, was for this under their director Karel Bendl, a fellow student of Dvořák at the Organ School. In those days, Dvořák had made extensive use of Bendl's library of music and often practised the piano at his house.

Karel Bendl (1838-1897).

Dvořák was by now again working hard on chamber music, none of which was destined to be published until long after his death. A Piano Quintet in A is dated 1872. In the following year he completed two more String Quartets, one in F minor (originally Opus 9) and one in A minor (Opus 12), the latter not to be confused with another in the same key, written in 1874 and published the following year as Opus 16.

From April to July 1873 he devoted his time to the most ambitious of his compositions to date, a Third Symphony, and the only one of his nine symphonies not in the customary four movements (the scherzo is omitted). Smetana conducted the première at a

Philharmonic concert on 30 March, 1874.

On 17 November the previous year, Dvořák had married nineteen-year old Anna Čermáková, a former pupil and subsequently a contralto in the Opera Chorus and the younger sister of his previous love, Josefina. In this respect he was following the example set by Haydn and Mozart, both of whom married sisters of women who had rejected them.

It seems that the success of Dvořák's *The Heirs of the White Mountain* earlier in the year had finally overcome the opposition of Anna's parents. For the first three months after the wedding the couple lived with the Čermák family, and despite the loss of three children the marriage proved to be one of great happiness (Anna Dvořák survived her husband, and died at the age of seventy-seven in 1931).

At this time, Dvořák relinquished his post in the Opera orchestra and, in January 1874, was in succession to his teacher Josef Foerster, appointed organist at St. Adalbert's Church. For this he received an annual salary of 126 gulden, scarcely more than he had been earning as a viola player. In that same month he began his Fourth Symphony, completing it in March. Although Smetana performed the scherzo on 25 May, 1875, the whole Symphony was not heard until March, 1892 when it was given in Prague under the composer's baton.

Dvořák decided to submit both the Third and Fourth Symphonies for a prize offered by the Austrian Government to assist 'young poor and talented artists'. As part of his application, he was obliged to provide a certificate proving that he qualified for the award:

The Town Clerk's Office of the Royal Capital of Prague hereby confirms, for the purpose of gaining a State grant, due official investigations having been made, that Antonín Dvořák, teacher of music, born in 1841, married and father of one unprovided child, has no property, and that, except for a salary of 126 gulden which he receives as organist of the Church of St. Adalbert and 60 gulden which he earns monthly by private music teaching, he has no other source of income.

Prague   24.6.1874

The adviser of the Music Department of the Austrian Government was the Viennese critic Eduard Hanslick

Vitězslav Hálek, author of *Evening Songs* and *Heirs of the White Mountain,* to which Dvořák composed his *Hymnus,* Op. 30.

29

The composer's wife,
Anna Čermáková.

St. Adalbert Church, Prague.

Dvořák's first home in Prague.

(1825-1904), noted for his support of the music of Brahms. Dvořák's application was successful and in February 1875, he was awarded a prize of 400 gulden.

On Christmas Eve, 1874, Dvořák completed a one-act comic opera with the title *The Pig-Headed Peasants*. The plot is rather like *Romeo and Juliet* in reverse: because of their parents' encouragement, a boy and a girl *refuse* to acknowledge that they are in love with each other. Only through jealousy aroused by the old village gossip is the problem resolved.

The first performance was delayed until October, 1881 when the opera was produced at the Provisional Theatre. A poor presentation on stage caused it to be withdrawn and it received no further performances during the composer's lifetime.

1875 was for Dvořák an even more active year for composition, with the completion of the *Nocturne*, the Serenade in E (both scored for string orchestra) and the Fifth Symphony (published, confusingly, as the third). Chamber works included the first Piano Trio in B flat, a String Quintet in G and a Piano Quartet in D.

The second half of the year was devoted to Dvořák's most ambitious project, thus far, the five-act grand opera *Vanda*. The story relates how a Polish princess swears to sacrifice herself if her people defeat the invading Germans. A poor libretto failed, however, to inspire the composer and after the initial four performances in April 1876, the work was not revived until 1929 when it was staged in Prague.

The only sadness at this time was the death of the Dvořáks' two-day-old daughter, Josefa, on 21 September 1875. A second Piano Trio in G minor, completed the following year, expresses the composer's grief. The same month he began work on a setting of the sombre *Stabat Mater*.

Early in 1876, Dvořák began to teach Marie Neffová, the wife of Jan Neff, a Moravian businessman and a great lover of music. The three often performed vocal duets with piano accompaniment, but soon found themselves growing tired of the limited repertoire of German songs. At Neff's suggestion Dvořák composed for soprano and tenor his first set of four *Moravian Duets*. So well did these go, that in the summer of that year he completed a second set of fourteen duets, this time for soprano and contralto,

31

Johannes Brahms.

followed by a further set of four songs.

All but one of the songs from the second set were published privately at Neff's expense with some copies handsomely bound and distributed to leading musicians and critics. According to Marie Neffová, one of these was sent, without Dvořák's knowledge, to Brahms.

Brahms had replaced Johann Herbeck, director of the *Hofoper*, on the adjudicating board of the Austrian State Commission that considered applications for the grant which had been awarded to Dvořák in the previous year. Brahms was much impressed by the *Moravian Duets*, and wrote an enthusiastic letter to the publisher Simrock:

Dear S.

In connection with the State grant, I have for several years past had great pleasure in the works of Antonín Dvořák (pronounced Dworschak) in Prague. This year he sent in,

among other things, a volume of Duets for two sopranos with piano accompaniment, which seems to be very practical for publication. The volume appears to have been printed at the composer's own expense. The title, and unfortunately also the texts are in Czech only. I have advised him to send you the songs. When you play them over you will, like me, be delighted with their piquant charm. It would be necessary, however, to see to obtaining a very good translation. Dvořák has written all sorts of things: operas (Czech), symphonies, quartets, and piano music. There is no doubt that he is very talented. And then he is also poor. I beg you to think the matter over. The Duets won't give you much thought and will sell well.

With best greetings,

Yours,

J.Br.

Fritz Simrock (1837-1901), Dvořák's publisher, played an important part in the composer's career. They met frequently in Karlovy Vary (Carlsbad).

Up to that time (apart from a handful of privately published pieces), only one solitary song and a String Quartet of Dvořák's were in print. Neff's publication of the *Moravian Duets* helped to maintain the government grant which Dvořák received in all for five years. Newly glossed with German texts, the *Duets* were then published by Simrock early in 1878, thereby providing a European market for a composer whose music had hitherto circulated only in Prague.

Dvořák's other major work of 1876 was the Piano Concerto in G minor, Opus 33, written in August and September. This was first performed by Karel Slavkovský in Prague in March 1878 (an English première followed at the Crystal Palace in October, 1883 with Oscar Beringer as soloist). Although Dvořák had written for the piano as a solo instrument and in chamber music and songs, he seemed less able to provide a virtuoso piece for piano and orchestra. The piano writing is often awkwardly laid out, and concert pianists have, on the whole, avoided performing the work. A revised version by Wilém Kurz alters the piano part considerably in places but neither this nor the original has been widely played. In recent years, a number of leading pianists have revived the concerto but its popularity remains limited.

In February 1877, Dvořák relinquished his post as organist at St. Adalbert's Church in order to devote more time to composition. Almost immediately, he

The programme of the first performance of *The Peasant, a Rogue,* given in Prague in 1878.

Four years later, the opera received its first performance outside the country at the Dresden Theatre.

began work on his sixth opera, *The Peasant, a Rogue,* the plot of which concerns the attempts of Martin, a rich peasant, to marry his daughter Bětuška to Václav when she is in love with Jeńik. This aspect of the story seems related to *The Bartered Bride.* Another opera, Mozart's *The Marriage of Figaro,* is called to mind when the Prince discovers that the woman he is seducing is not Bětuška, but his own wife in disguise.

The première at the provisional Theatre on 27 January 1878 was a triumph for the composer, and performances followed in Dresden (1882), Hamburg (1883) and Vienna (1885).

Chapter 5

Brahms

'There is no doubt that he (Dvořák) is very talented. And then he is also poor'—Brahms

In 1877, further tragedies struck the Dvořák household. On 13 August, their ten-month-old daughter Růžena died, followed within the month by the death on 8 September of their son Otakar, aged three.

Dvořák's setting of the *Stabat Mater*, begun after the death of baby Josefa, was completed in November 1877 and now becoming a poignant memorial to all three children. The Quartet in D minor Opus 34, written in the last month of that year, also expresses the grief that deeply affected the composer.

In a letter to Brahms, dated 23 January 1878, Dvořák asked permission to dedicate the Quartet to him:

Brahms at the piano: drawing by W. von Bechrath.

Honoured Master,

About three weeks ago I set out on my intended journey to Vienna in order to thank you personally for all the kindness that you have shown me. I was very sorry that I was not fortunate enough to see you before you left for Leipzig. I took the opportunity to visit Professor Hanslick who received me very cordially. At his request, I left a number of my compositions with your housekeeper and beg you, if you are already back in Vienna, to be so good as to look them through. At the same time I take the liberty of inquiring whether you received the Duets with the German translation and whether it is good.

Mr. Simrock wrote to me a few days ago. He will be pleased to publish the Duets, only a number of places must be changed for the sake of declamation.

I have further the honour to inform you that your splendid D minor Concerto was performed at a concert

String Quartet in
E major, Op. 27/80.

given recently here in Prague and was extremely successful.

And now I venture, highly honoured Master, to approach you with a request. Permit me, out of gratitude and a deep respect for your incomparable musical works, to offer you the dedication of my D minor Quartet.

It would be for me the highest honour I can aspire to and I should be the happiest of men to subscribe myself as bound to you in eternal gratitude and

Your devoted Servant,
Antonín Dvořák

Brahms had been on a concert tour of Germany and Holland, conducting his first two Symphonies. On his return to Vienna in March, he replied to Dvořák's letter:

37

Dear Sir,

I regret extremely that I was away from home when you were here, the more so as I have an aversion to letter-writing that I cannot hope to make up for it in the least by correspondence. And today, no more than to say that to occupy myself with your pieces gives me the greatest pleasure, but that I would give a good deal to be able to discuss individual points with you personally. You write somewhat hurriedly. When you are filling in the numerous missing sharps, flats and naturals, then it would be good to look a little more closely at the notes themselves and at the voice parts, etc.

Forgive me, but it is very desirable to point out such things to a man like you. I also accept the works just as they are, very gratefully and consider myself honoured by the dedication of the quartet.

I think it would be very good if you gave me both the quartets that I know. If Simrock should not be willing, might I try to place them elsewhere?

Accept once more my best thanks for your news and warm greetings from

Your entirely devoted
J. Brahms.

Facsimile of a letter from Brahms to Dvořák written in 1879.

The E major Quartet, Opus 27, composed in 1876, was accepted by Simrock, but issued as Opus 80. The D minor Quartet was published by Schlesinger in Berlin.

In a letter to Simrock, dated 5 May, 1878, Brahms again wrote supporting Dvořák's music:

I do not know what further risk you are wanting to take with this man. I have no idea about business matters or what interest there is for larger works. I do not care to make recommendations, because I have only my eyes and my ears and they are altogether my own. If you should think of going on with it all, get him to send you his two string quartets, major and minor, and have them played to you. The best that a musician can have, Dvořák has, and it is in these compositions. I am an incorrigible philistine. I should publish even my own works for the pleasure of it.

In short I cannot say anything more than that I recommend Dvořák in general and particular. Besides, you have your own ears and business sense to guide you.

The friendship between Dvořák and Brahms survived unbroken until the death in 1897 of the older man. In many respects they were quite different personalities. A devout Catholic, Dvořák had little in common with Brahms, a lapsed Protestant, latterly an agnostic. Dvořák was happily married, a family man, Brahms an increasingly crusty bachelor. The stormy temperament of Brahms expressed in his early compositions, in the First Piano Concerto and the F minor Piano Quintet in particular, has no counterpart in the works of Dvořák. The passionate lyrical quality of the music of both composers, however, developed along similar lines, and although Brahms wrote no operas or symphonic poems, the musical forms they used were often similar.

The instant success, in Germany especially, of the *Moravian Duets* led Simrock to commission from Dvořák a set of *Slavonic Dances*. These, he clearly hoped, would match in popularity the *Hungarian Dances* of Brahms. Like these, the *Slavonic Dances* were

Dvořák's orchestral arrangement of Brahms' Hungarian Dance, No. 17.

Dvořák in 1879.

composed initially for piano duet, a form in which they would achieve the widest sales as they could be played in almost every home. The brilliant orchestra version was completed shortly afterwards. It is sobering to note that on their publication in August 1878, Dvořák received just 300 marks, a tiny sum of money compared to the fortune that Simrock was to earn from them over the succeeding years.

Also dating from this time is the genial Serenade in D minor for wind instruments, 'cello and doublebass, composed within a fortnight in January 1878. Dvořák dedicated this to Louis Ehlert, a German music critic who had written an enthusiastic notice of his music in the Berlin newspaper *Die Neue Musikzeitung*. The Serenade was first performed by players from the Provisional Theatre Orchestra in the following November. Three *Slavonic Rhapsodies* (again from 1878) were well received by audiences in Prague and Vienna but have since become overshadowed by the more popular *Slavonic Dances*.

On 14 May, Dvořák made the acquaintance of the

famed violinist Joseph Joachim at the latter's home. As a result, the Joachim Quartet gave the première of his Sextet in A, Opus 48. The following year, they also gave the first performance of the Quartet in E flat, Opus 50.

On 12 December, Dvořák travelled by train from Prague to Vienna to meet Brahms for the first time, taking with him the score of the D minor Quartet.

The speed of Dvořák's rise to international fame can have had little parallel. Within two years, the obscure composer from Prague had become honoured throughout Germany and Austria and his music had even reached England.

In May, 1879 he started work on the Violin Concerto in A minor. Two months later he again visited Joachim, this time to seek advice on the solo part. Unlike Brahms, Dvořák was a violinist and could therefore write for the instrument from first-hand experience. He did nevertheless adopt Joachim's suggestions for alterations, and after completing the score in September, sent the music to Joachim.

In a letter to Simrock dated 9 May, 1880, Dvořák indicated to what extent he had revised the Concerto:

In accordance with Mr. Joachim's wishes, I have most

Josef Joachim was a great admirer of Dvořák and championed his works throughout Europe, both as a distinguished soloist and as leader of the Joachim Quartet.

František Ondříček
(1859-1922).

Hans Richter.

carefully worked over the entire Concerto without missing a single bar. The whole work has been transformed. Although I have retained some themes, I have written several new ones. The whole concept of the work is however changed. The harmonization, the orchestration, the rhythms are new.

Evidently still unhappy, Joachim held on to the score for two years, making changes to the solo part and thereby delaying the première.

The first performance took place in Prague in October, 1883 with František Ondříček, who later presented the Concerto in Vienna under Hans Richter. The English première was also given by Ondříček in April, 1886. On that occasion the *Musical Times* review was most favourable:

The Concerto was very finely played, beauty of tone, truth of phrasing, and facility of execution being revealed in the highest degree throughout the work, the close of the piece producing a perfect storm of applause, and the performer being recalled amidst much enthusiasm.

Following the Violin Concerto, Dvořák wrote the Violin Sonata in F, Opus 57, a work surprisingly neglected in the limited repertoire of Romantic chamber works for the instrument.

Between August and October 1880, he completed the Symphony in D, Opus 58, published in 1882 as the First, but now known correctly as the Sixth. This was dedicated to Hans Richter who became an enthusiastic champion of Dvořák's music. The first performance was conducted by Adolf Čech, the composer's friend from student days, at a concert in Prague in March, 1881.

The D major Symphony was first heard in England in March of the following year, when it was played at London's Crystal Palace conducted by August Manns. In 1884 the Symphony reached New York where it was performed under the father of American music-making, Theodore Thomas.

For his next project, Dvořák returned to the domestic piano duet, completing early in 1881 ten *Legends*, an orchestral version following at Simrock's request in December.

In spite of the failure of his historical tragedy *Vanda*, Dvořák did not hesitate once he had received the

Dvořák's friend, Alois Göbl (1841-1907), was secretary to Prince Rohan who lived at Sychrov Castle.

libretto to begin work on his next opera *Dimitri*. The text, by Marie Červinková-Riegrová the daughter of an eminent politician Dr. František Rieger, was based on several sources including Schiller and Ostrovsky. It had been originally given to another composer, Karel Šebor (1843-1903), a friend of Dvořák's, but the long delay in starting on the music prompted the author to ask for the text to be returned.

Dimitri, who falsely claimed to be the son of Ivan the Terrible, succeeded Boris Godunov as Tsar of Russia, but was deposed by the boyars. At the time of composing the music, Dvořák did not know Mussorgsky's opera *Boris Godunov*. 'Prince' Dimitri, with the support of Polish troops, enters Moscow with his wife, Marina, a Polish princess. He falls in love with Xenie, the daughter of Boris, whom he has rescued. When Xenie learns that Dimitri was her father's enemy, she enters a convent. The jealous Marina, denounces Dimitri as an impostor and he is

Scene from the opera
Dimitri, 1882.

murdered by Shuisky, the chief minister of Boris.

The opera occupied Dvořák for an unusually long time. Although the piano score was finished after five months in May, 1881, he did not complete the orchestration until September 1882. The première had been intended for the Czech National Theatre but this building was burnt down in August, 1881. The first performance on 8 October, 1882 conducted by Mořic Anger in the New Czech Theatre, Prague was a triumph. The critics were also generous in their praise, although Hanslick expressed doubts about the libretto. Dvořák subsequently made alterations to the fourth act and added some colourful ballet, the revised version being presented on 28 November, 1885.

In spite of its popularity at home, where the opera received over fifty performances before the end of the century, *Dimitri* was never produced abroad, except in Vienna where it was staged, once, in 1892. While living in America, Dvořák continued to make further changes in the music but the work failed to achieve any wider acceptance.

Chapter 6

Dvořák and Simrock

'I shall simply do what God tells me to do, that will certainly be the best thing'—Dvořák to Simrock

In 1879, Dvořák signed a contract with the publisher Simrock, agreeing to offer him all his new compositions before seeking publication elsewhere.

Like every businessman, Simrock had first and foremost to consider the commercial possibilities of any music that was offered to him. He had made astute decisions, for example, in issuing the *Moravian Duets* and commissioning the *Slavonic Dances*, both of which earned him a fortune, although the composer's share was minimal.

Dvořák's first conflict with Simrock arose over what might seem a trivial irritation. Dvořák insisted that his Christian name should be printed as Ant., the abbreviation for Antonín, and not as Anton, the German form of his name. When Simrock ignored the composer's request, Dvořák wrote a forceful letter, dated 22 August, 1885:

Don't make fun of my Czech brothers and don't feel sorry for me either. What I ask of you is only a wish, and if you are unable to grant it, then I have a right to regard that as an unkindness the like of which I have never found with either English or French publishers.

Simrock's continuing unwillingness to accede to Dvořák's demand served merely to increase the composer's anger. In a letter of 10 September, 1887 he expressed his feelings as a Czech musician:

And let us hope the nations never perish which possess art

and represent it, however small they are. Forgive me for this, but I simply wish to tell you that an artist also has a homeland in which he must have faith and to which he must always have a warm heart.

Although he did not associate with any extreme Czech national organisation and took no part in politics, Dvořák was strongly conscious of his national identity and resisted any attempts to Germanicize what was essentially Bohemian or Moravian. He wished only that if the titles of his pieces were to be printed in German and Czech, the words of his songs should also appear in both languages. As further evidence of his strong sense of nationality, Dvořák refused in London in August 1885, an invitation to dine at the Club of German Artists, declaring that he was not a German.

As his fame grew, Dvořák, probably with the prompting of his wife, pressed for better terms from his publisher. Although Simrock continued to make money from Dvořák's music, he pointed out that large-scale works did not sell well and were costly to print. He still wished, however, to publish the Seventh Symphony in D minor, and offered 3000 marks for the score. At the same time, he urged Dvořák to provide him with a second set of *Slavonic Dances*.

On 18 May, 1885 Dvořák replied:

I fully recognise the validity of the points you put forward, that is from the business point of view. I, again, from mine, must draw attention to important considerations which I am sure you will also respect.

1. If I give you the Symphony for 3000M, then I have as good as lost 3000M, because another firm offers me this sum, in which case I should be very sorry if your should wish to force me, so to speak, into such a situation.
2. I think that even though such large works do not produce the desired financial results straight away, the time may come when everything will be amply made up for, and
3. I beg you to consider that in my *Slavonic Dances* you have found a gold mine which cannot be easily underestimated and
4. If I take and consider all that you indicated in your last letter from a commonsense point of view, then we reach a very simple conclusion; not to write symphonies and large vocal and instrumental works, but only publish here and there some songs, piano pieces and dances and I know not

View of Prague
overlooking the Vltava
towards St. Vitus
Cathedral.

what else; this, as an artist who wants to make his mark, I cannot do.

Yes my friend, you see that is how I look upon it from my artistic point of view, and I hope you will appreciate mine as I do yours. This, however does lead to some conclusions. If you do not wish, or rather, if you simply cannot give me these 6000M then all talking and writing comes to an end; what difference is it between you and me if you have 3000M less and I by so much more. Remember, I pray you, that I am a poor artist and the father of a family and do not wrong me.

With warm greetings,
Your sincere friend,
Ant. Dvořák

Simrock had in 1880 paid only 2000 marks for the Sixth Symphony, but under Dvořák's entreaties he agreed to the 6000 marks asked for the new Symphony in D minor. Two choral works commissioned by

47

No. 14 Žitná ulice,
where Dvořák lived
from 1877.

Charles Square, with
the St. Ignace Church
(foreground).

Novello, *The Spectre's Bride* (1884) and *St. Ludmilla* (1886) were published by that firm in the respective years following their composition.

Good relations were restored between composer and publisher with a second set of *Slavonic Dances*, for which Dvořák was able to extract 3000 marks: ten times what he had received for the first set, but a fair price in view of the money Simrock had already made from the earlier work.

In the autumn of 1887, Dvořák travelled to Berlin where he sold Simrock six works for the total payment of 6000 marks. Five of them were relatively early pieces: the Symphony in F, published as the third but now numbered as five, the String Quintet in G Opus 77, the Symphonic Variations, a setting for chorus and orchestra of Psalm 149 and the String Quartet in E, Opus 80. Of these, only the Piano Quintet in A, Opus 81, was a recent composition.

Within a few years Simrock was again complaining that he had lost money on the larger works and was begging Dvořák to compose piano pieces and songs that were commercially so much more lucrative and less expensive to produce.

In a letter of 3 January, 1890, Simrock wrote:

If only I did sufficient business with your symphonies to be repaid for the enormous expense. But this is far from the case and I am thousands down on them. What use is it if I make money on one or six works and lose it again on four others? I cannot carry on business like that! If the performances are successful the composer always thinks his work will sell. You were successful here over Bülow's performance of your D minor symphony but subsequently not a single copy, not even a piano duet version, was sold. So unless you also give me small and easy piano pieces, it won't be possible to publish big works.

Dvořák took this as an outright refusal to accept the larger compositions. On 7 October he replied:

Since you have thought it right once more to reject my symphony I shall not offer you any big expensive works in future, for I shall know in advance, because of what you say, that you cannot publish such works. You advise me to write small works: but that is difficult, for how can I help it if no theme for a song or a piano piece comes to my head? Just now my mind is full of big ideas—I shall do as God wills.

A drawing of Antonín Dvořák by Hugo Boettinger.

Dvořák ignored Simrock's reminder of the 1879 agreement. No further correspondence passed between them for over a year. As the composer had waited twelve months and more to hear if Simrock would accept the Mass in D, he offered it instead to Novello who published it in 1893. They also issued in 1892 the Eighth Symphony.

Yet in a letter dated 25 November, 1891 to his friend Alóis Göbl, Secretary to Prince Rohan at Sychrov, Dvořák wrote:

Simrock has remembered my existence; he was probably sorry at not having heard anything about me for so long. He would like to have something again, but I am letting him wait in the meantime to punish him. If he doesn't pay me very well, I shan't give him either the 'Overtures' or the 'Dumky'. I shall always be able to get them accepted. I won't allow myself to be done down by him anymore.

Time seemed to heal the damaged relations between the two men. From Spillville, Iowa on 28 July, 1893, Dvořák wrote a friendly letter to Simrock giving details of his compositions and offering them to him with suggested figures for payment:

Dear Friend. I am composing now, thank goodness, only for my pleasure. I am fairly independent, have a salary of 15,000 dollars and so am able to devote my leisure to composing and am content. I am therefore in no hurry to publish my works. If you recollect your correspondence in Prague two years ago, you will easily understand why I am holding off publishing my works.

All the works you could have (with the exception of the not yet complete Quintet) if we could agree on the fee. The Overtures (1, 2, 3) for 2000M, the Dumky, 2000M, the E minor Symphony 2000M, the Rondo (Cello solo) 500M, altogether 6,500M. The title, inside as well, should be in both German and Czech.

I am not asking any more than what you have always paid me.

Antonín Dvořák

To avoid delay and possible loss in sending the music across the Atlantic, Brahms offered to proof-read these works. This act of extreme generosity moved Dvořák deeply. Proof-reading is for any composer a tedious chore, and to spend valuable time

Sophia Island (now known as Slavonic Island) in Prague where a number of Dvořák's works including the *Symphonic Variations* (1877) were given their first performances.

away from composition in order to correct the printed copies of music by another shows the high regard Brahms held for his younger friend.

In a letter to Simrock on 5 February, 1894, Dvořák wrote simply:

I can scarcely believe there is another composer in the world who would do as much.

One further gold mine was to come to Simrock. Back at Vysoká in August, 1894, during the vacation between his two visits to America, Dvořák composed for piano a set of *Humoresques*. Sensing their possible popularity, Simrock paid the high sum of 4,000 marks, a figure soon justified as the seventh *Humoresque* became quickly Dvořák's single most widely performed work, spawning a multitude of arrangements. With the money, Dvořák bought an organ for the church at Vysoká which was installed on his birthday, 8 September, 1894.

Chapter 7

Dvořák in England

'How very big it is . . . if all the inhabitants of Kladno were to visit that enormous hall, there would still be plenty of room'—Dvořák to his father

The March 1879 issue of the London journal, *The Monthly Musical Record*, reviewed a performance of some of the *Slavonic Dances*, probably the first of Dvořák's music to be heard in Britain:

There is considerable amount of fascination in the melancholy tone of the melodies of these Slavonian Dances, and the constant change of rhythm and the alternation of slow and rapid movements has an effect not at all unpleasing. There is no great pretension in the work as a musical composition other than that which aims at the representation of a national peculiarity, and the reproduction, in a quasi-classical form, of things that are in their origin popular.

Dvořák's passport.

In 1880 the *Slavonic Dances* were heard at Crystal Palace, and in the same year the String Sextet in A was twice performed at St. James's Hall.

An article on Dvořák's music by the critic Joseph Bennet in the *Musical Times* for April and May, 1881 helped to inform musicians, and publication of the *Stabat Mater* by Novello in 1883 firmly established him as a composer of some reputation. Joseph Barnby conducted the work in the Royal Albert Hall on 16 March with the London Musical Society.

Henry Littleton, the head of Novello, Ewer and Co., and secretary to the Philharmonic Society of London, subsequently sent a letter to Dvořák in August 1883, inviting him to London for three concerts of his music. On 5 March, 1884, Dvořák set out from Prague with a

51

Henry Littleton, head of the well-known publishing house of Novello, Ewer & Co.

friend, the pianist Jindřich Káan, travelling by way of Cologne and Brussels. On their arrival in London on 8 March, they were met by the pianist Oscar Beringer, with whom Dvořák was to stay, and Henry Littleton.

The English newspapers gave the Czech composer a welcome similar to the reception that greeted Haydn when he first set foot in London almost a century earlier. At the first concert on 13 March, Dvořák conducted the *Stabat Mater*. In a letter to the Prague critic and publisher Valebín Urbánek, he described the overwhelming impression made upon him by the size of the Royal Albert Hall and by the forces involved in the performance.

On Monday there was the first rehearsal with the choir in the Albert Hall, an immense building which can comfortably seat 12,000 people. When I appeared at the desk, I was welcomed with such a thunder of applause that it took some considerable time before there was quiet again. I was so deeply touched with the warmth of the ovation that I could not speak a word, and, in any case, it would not have been any use as nobody would have understood me.

I must, however, give you an idea of the size of the orchestra and choir. Don't get a shock! 250 sopranos, 160 contraltos, 180 tenors and 250 basses; the orchestra; 24 first violins, 20 second violins, 16 violas, 16 cellos and 16 double-basses.

The effect of such an immense corpus was truly magnificent. It is, indeed, indescribable.

Two days before the concert, Littleton gave a dinner in the composer's honour to which 150 guests were invited. There followed a concert of his music that lasted into the early hours of the morning, which must have proved exhausting for one who preferred, as a rule, to retire early.

Littleton's house at Sydenham, a London suburb.

53

The Royal Albert Hall,
London.

The *Stabat Mater* was another great success.

At the concert my appearance was greeted with a storm of applause. The general enthusiasm grew from item to item, and, at the end, the applause was so great that I had to thank the audience again and again. At the same time the orchestra and choir overwhelmed me from the other side with the heartiest ovations. In short it turned out better than I could ever have hoped for.

Dvořák was astonished at the size of London and was characteristically interested in the complex railway system of the capital. In a letter dated 21 March to his father, he attempted to convey some of his impressions:

Just to give you a slight idea of what this London looks like and how very big it is, I shall tell you the following:
If all the Czech inhabitants of the whole of Bohemia were put together, they would not number as many as the inhabitants of London. And if all the inhabitants of Kladno were to visit that enormous hall where I conducted by *Stabat*

54

Mater, there would still be plenty of room,—for that is how huge the Albert Hall is.

In the same letter he reported that:

In some papers there was also mention made of you, that I came from poor parents and that my father was a butcher and innkeeper in Nelahozeves and did everything to give his son a proper education. Honour be to you for that!

The people of London, where Dvořák was the lion of

Dvořák and his wife in London.

the musical season, took the composer to their hearts. Three banquets were arranged for him and newspapers and journals carried lengthy articles about him. One critic, Herman Klein, described him vividly as being 'simple as a child, his dark piercing eyes rarely lighting up with a smile . . . A crushing handshake'.

At the second concert on 20 March at St. James's Hall, Dvořák conducted *The Hussites* Overture, the Sixth Symphony, the Second *Slavonic Rhapsody* and two of the *Gypsy Songs*, sung in English by the tenor W. J. Winch, with the composer at the piano. The songs were repeated two days later at Crystal Palace, where they shared a programme with the *Nocturne* for strings and the lively *Scherzo Capriccioso*.

Dvořák returned to Prague on 29 March with a commission in his pocket from the Birmingham Musical Festival for a choral work at a fee of £2,000. On 14 June, the Philharmonic Society of Lodon elected him an honorary member and asked him to write a Symphony for them.

In the autumn of 1884, Dvořák returned to England to conduct at the Three Choirs Festival in Worcester, described by him in a letter to his father as 'Worcester, a big industrial town' (he seems, in fact, to have been thinking of Birmingham). Henry Littleton met him at Dover and took him to his mansion in Sydenham, close to the Crystal Palace. There he was introduced to the American composer Dudley Buck, who invited him to undertake a concert tour of the United States.

On the morning of 11 September he conducted the *Stabat Mater*. The distinguished soloists were Madame Emma Albani, Janet Patey, Edward Lloyd and Charles Santley. The London and provincial critics were greatly impressed by the work, and it became further established in the English choral repertoire. At the evening concert on the same day, Dvořák conducted his Sixth Symphony. One of the first violins on that occasion was the twenty-seven year old Edward Elgar, and in a letter dated 28 September 1884 to his friend Percy Buck, Elgar wrote:

I wish your could hear Dvořák's music. It is simply ravishing, so tuneful and clever and the orchestration is wonderful; no matter how few instruments he uses, it never sounds thin; I cannot describe it; it must be heard.

The title page of the
manuscript of the *Stabat
Mater*, Op. 21.

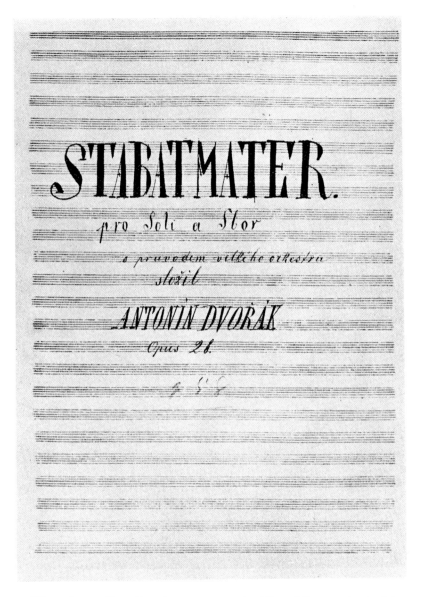

The day after the two concerts, Dvořák wrote to his wife:

Yesterday I again had a great day. *Stabat Mater* in the wonderful and very large church (4000 people) made a tremendous impression. It was the finest day of the whole celebrations as everybody here was saying. When we left the church, everybody was looking at me and everybody would have liked to shake hands with me and say a few words, which of course was not possible with such a large number of people.

Everywhere I appear, whether in the street or at home or even when I go into a shop to buy something, people crowd

Crystal Palace,
Sydenham, destroyed
by fire in 1936.

round me and ask for my autograph. There are pictures of
me at all the booksellers and people buy them only to have
some memento.

After returning to Prague he began sketching the
Symphony (his seventh) for the Philharmonic Society:
the scoring occupied him from December to March of
the following year.

Dvořák's third visit to England lasted a month. He
conducted to great acclaim the première of the new
Symphony at a Philharmonic Concert on 22 April 1885
in St. James's Hall. At the next Philharmonic Concert
on 6 May, Franz Rummel played the Piano Concerto
under the composer's direction.

Also in St. James's Hall, on 13 May, Dvořák
conducted the Geaussent Choir in the revised version
of *The Heirs of the White Mountain*, recently published
by Novello, and now known as *Hymnus*.

The Spectre's Bride, the cantata commissioned by the
Birmingham Musical Festival, was composed between
May and November, 1884. The text was by the Czech
poet Karl Jaromir Erban, taken from his *Bouquet of Folk
Tales* published in 1853. The legend is found in several
sources, and in the version by G. A. Burger entitled
Leonore, it inspired a symphony by Raff and a
symphonic poem by Duparc, the story telling of a lover
who returns to his bride and reveals himself as a corpse

58

leading her to her grave. Only repentance and prayer save her from death.

Not everything ran smoothly. When Dvořák learnt that Gounod was to receive 100,000 francs for his oratorio *Mors et Vita* for the same Festival, he wrote to Littleton:

Pray to not pay Mr. Gounod who truly does not need it, so immense sums, for what would be left for me?

In the event, Gounod was paid the money but failed to arrive to conduct the work.

Although Birmingham had commissioned *The Spectre's Bride*, the first performance was given in Plzeň by the Hlahol Choral Society under the composer on 28 March 1885. He had also intended conducting performances in Olomouc and Prague in May but, as he was still in England, his place was taken by his friend, Karel Bendl.

Dvořák arrived in London on 17 August and travelled the same day to Birmingham for a rehearsal in the evening. He returned to London the following day, continuing with Henry Littleton his journey to a house

Dvořák composed *The Spectre's Bride* for the 1884 Birmingham Festival using as his text a ballad by the Czech poet K. J. Erben.

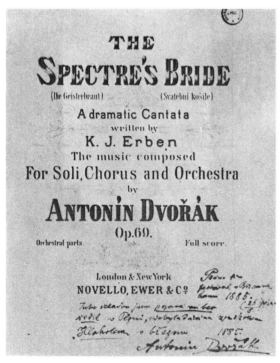

59

in Brighton where the composer was surprised but delighted to see English ladies bathing publicly beside the men and children.

Before going to Birmingham for the performance, he rehearsed the orchestra in London. The concert took place on 27 August with a choir of 500 and an orchestra of 150. Once again, the young Elgar was one of the first violins, and the soloists were Albani, Josef Maas and Santley.

To his friend, Alois Göbl, Dvořák wrote:

I am here in this immense industrial town where they make excellent knives, scissors, springs, files and I don't know what else, and besides these, music too. And how well. It is terrible what the people here manage to do and to stand! There will be eight concerts in all and each will last four to five hours. My day is Thursday 27th at 8 p.m. Please think of me!

The success of the cantata led in 1885 to performances as far apart as Manchester and Milwaukee, while the following year Edinburgh, Glasgow, London and Melbourne, Australia also heard *The Spectre's Bride*. For over fifty years it remained a firm favourite with choral societies in Britain.

Later in 1885, Dvořák began work on the Leeds Festival commission. The text of *St. Ludmilla* was by the Czech poet, Jaroslav Vrchlický, the pseudonym of

The banner of the Hlahol Choral Society.

The headquarters of the Hlahol Choral Society.

Emil Frïida, and tells of the coming of Christianity to Bohemia in the Ninth Century. The Leeds Festival committee expressed some doubts as to the suitability of the subject but the composer would not change his mind.

Finished in May, 1886, the oratorio was planned with Handel's *Messiah* very much in mind, and is consequently divided into forty-five separate movements. Accompanied by his wife, Dvořák set out for England on 1 October.

The first performance, at which soloists were again Albani, Patey, Lloyd and Santley, took place in Leeds on 15 October. Once more the composer experienced a triumph. Writing to his friend, Antonín Rus, a judge who lived near Vysoká, he said:

At last everything is over: my victory was tremendous and I hasten to give you more details.

St. Ludmilla made in general a great impression and was the high point of the whole festival as all the London newspapers write and which you will read in our papers in a few days. Such a choir and orchestra as is here I have not heard in England yet. It was magnificent. But all words are vain. The welcome I got from the audience, the choir and

61

Jaroslav Vrchlický
(1853-1912).

From the National
Theatre production of
St. Ludmila in 1901.

the orchestra was so hearty and sincere that I was carried off
my feet.

During the performance, nearly every number was
received with storms of applause, and at the end of Part I,
the audience, choir and orchestra broke out into such cheers
that I felt quite queer.

After it ended the calls for Dvořák seemed interminable
and I said a few words to the audience in English and
thanked them for their warm welcome and the excellent
performance of my work, which again called forth new
storms of applause. In short it was a great day on which I
shall always look back with joy.

The critic of the London *Times* was less enthusiastic:

His (Dvořák's) attempts at dramatic characterisation are of
the feeblest kind and his dialogue whether carried on in
'recitativo secco' or obbligato is, with few exceptions,
conventional and uninteresting. Of declamatory effects in
the modern sense, he has not the faintest glimmering. On

Leeds Town Hall.

A contemporary
caricature of Sir Arthur
Sullivan.

the other hand, his orchestration is always masterly and his sense of the musically picturesque is keener than that of any living composer, especially when he is able to take his local colour from the national songs and dance rhythms of his native Bohemia.

At the rehearsals, Arthur Sullivan had acted as interpreter for the composer.

Performances of *St. Ludmilla*, dedicated, it is interesting to discover, to the Zerotin Choral Union of Olomouc, followed in London at St. James's Hall and at Crystal Palace on, respectively, 29 October and 6 November. Dvořák conducted four more presentations of it in Prague in the following spring.

Over three years elapsed before Dvořák returned again to London. Then, on 24 April 1890 he conducted the English première of the Eighth Symphony, Opus 88. At the time, the conflict with Simrock was at its fiercest. When Dvořák was offered only 1000 marks for the Symphony, he placed it instead with Novello, who published it in 1892.

The composer's high esteem in England received recognition when, on the recommendation of the Professor of Music, Charles Villiers Stanford, Cambridge University conferred on him a Doctorate of Music.

Less than three weeks before the ceremony, Stanford was dismayed to receive a postcard written in English from the composer:

Sir Charles Villiers
Stanford (1852-1924).

My dear friend,
I hear from the London newspaper of today that there is
much influenza in your country and on account of that I and
my wife are afraid to come there. The journey from Prague
to London is very long and if we had a bad whether [sic] we
can easily take cold–and what shall we do then? Please tell
us, what is to be done?

Ever yours,
Ant. Dvořák

Stanford immediately telegraphed back reassuring
him that the newspaper was incorrect. Dvořák replied
on 30 May:

I with pleasure see that no danger is to the influenza.

On 15 June, 1891, the day before the ceremony, he
conducted performances of the *Stabat Mater* and the
new Symphony. Six others beside Dvořák received
honorary degrees on that occasion. These included the
Russian biologist Ilya Metchnikov, and the Irish
historian William Lecky.

64

Dvořák was evidently ill at ease at such a ceremony:

I shall never forget how I felt when they made me a doctor in England; the formalities and the doctors. All the faces so grave it seemed that no one could speak anything but Latin. I listened to my right and to my left and did not know where to turn my ear. And when I discovered that they were talking to me, I could have wished myself anywhere else than there and was ashamed that I did not know Latin. But when I look back on it I must smile and think to myself that to compose *Stabat Mater* is, after all, better than to know Latin.

Dvořák received an honorary doctorate from Cambridge University in 1891.

Hugo Becker, and
Ladislav Zelenka.

Dvořák and his wife were guests in Cambridge at Stanford's house. Stanford was rather put out by their lifelong habit of rising early:

I heard a noise in the garden in the small hours and found the pair sitting under a tree at 6 a.m.

Of the composer, Stanford wrote:

Dvořák did not show much interest in anything outside his own metier. He is one of the phenomena of the Nineteenth Century, a child of nature, who did not stop to think and said on paper anything which came in his mind.

After the success of *The Spectre's Bride*, the Birmingham Musical Festival commissioned from Dvořák a new composition for the 1888 season. One suggested subject was Cardinal Newman's poem *The Dream of Gerontius*. Newman had himself been in the audience at the performance of *The Spectre's Bride*, but Dvořák rejected *Gerontius* in favour of a setting of the Requiem Mass. In the event, work progressed slowly and Birmingham had to wait for a further three years. The piano score was completed by July 1890 and the orchestration occupied Dvořák from August until October. He conducted the first performance in Birmingham on 9 October 1891 and early the following year the *Requiem* was heard in Manchester, Liverpool and London. The Czech première took place on 12 March 1892 at Olomouc under the composer. He also conducted the first American performance, shortly after his arrival in the United States, in Boston on 3 November 1892.

For his ninth and final visit to England, Dvořák brought the Cello Concerto he had composed in New York. The work had been written for his friend Hanuš Wihan, but a disagreement over the cellist's wish to include a cadenza had caused some friction.

To Simrock, Dvořák wrote:

I shall only give you the work if you promise not to allow *anybody* to make changes, friend Wihan not excepted, without *my knowledge and consent*, and also not the cadenza

The famous German conductor and pianist Hans von Bülow once declared that ''the most important composer for me, apart from Brahms, is Dvořák''.

which Wihan had added to the last movement. There is no cadenza in the last movement, either in the score or in the piano arrangement. I told Wihan straight away when he showed it to me that it was impossible to stick such a bit on. The finale closes gradually *diminuendo*, like a sigh, with reminiscences of the 1st and 2nd movements, the solo dies down to *pp* (then swells again), and the last bars are taken up by the orchestra and the whole concludes in a stormy mood. That was my idea and I cannot depart from it.

As Wihan was unable to travel to London for the concert, the solo part was entrusted to the English cellist, Leo Stern who went to Prague to rehearse the work with the composer. The première took place on 19 March 1896 in London's Queen's Hall. Dvořák also conducted the Eighth Symphony and the *Biblical Songs*. Stern then travelled to Prague for the first Czech performance, on 11 April also under the composer's direction.

It only remains to record that the great success of Dvořák's last visit to London was a little offset by the appalling wet and windy weather, and by the fact that English food and English coffee were not at all to his liking.

Chapter 8

First Home

'If I ever become a rich man, or if ever I grow to be old, I will build a house with deep thatch to shelter me from the cold'—Hilaire Belloc

The death in Kladno, on 14 December 1882, of his mother, greatly affected Dvořák. As with the tragic loss of three of his children, he expressed his feelings in a chamber work, the F minor Piano Trio. Like the String Quartet in D minor, it possesses deep emotional moods seldom found in his orchestral writing. Although less well known than the *Dumky* Trio, composed seven years later, it is one of his finest compositions.

In the same year Dvořák completed two orchestral works. The *Scherzo Capriccioso* is an extended movement of joyous virtuosity, representing the composer at the height of his powers. It was first performed on 16 May 1863 under Adolf Čech, and subsequently conducted by the composer on many occasions in Prague, London and America.

The *Hussites* Overture, a tribute to the patriot Jan Hus, is a powerful statement of Dvořák's own strong nationalist sentiments. It was intended as the first part of a trilogy based on a subject suggested by František Adolf Šubert, Director of the Prague National Theatre, but the plan was never completed. The Overture was eventually heard at the opening ceremony of the newly rebuilt National Theatre on 18 November 1883, two years after the original Theatre had been razed to the ground.

The principal theme is, as we have seen, the Hussite hymn *Ye Warriors of God*, a rallying call to all Czechs, which Smetana had used as the basis of his symphonic

The first director of the National Theatre, F. A. Šubert, a close friend of Dvořák's.

The National Theatre,
Prague, opened in
November 1883, was
designed by Josef Zitek.

poems *Tabor* and *Blanik*. This fine overture was one of Dvořák's favourite works but it is seldom performed today.

For many years Dvořák had felt deeply disappointed that his operas had made such little impact abroad. They proved to be too nationalistic to gain a wide acceptance, and in 1884 he was offered two opera libretti in German by the *Generalintendant* at the Vienna Court Opera, Baron Hoffmann. At this time Brahms invited Dvořák to live in Vienna where his music was increasingly successful, but the homespun Bohemian had no wish to leave his homeland. The growing anti-Czech feeling in Vienna was already working against him and was partly responsible for the opposition to the production of his operas in the capital.

In a letter of 9 January 1886 to Bohumil Fidler composer, choirmaster and choral conductor in Příbram, he wrote:

70

The garden pavilion at Vysoká.

The auditorium of the National Theatre, Prague.

I am just a plain Czech musician, disliking such exaggerated humility and despite the fact that I have moved a little in the great musical world, I shall remain just what I was, a simple Czech musician.

In 1884, Dvořák was able to buy his first home. He purchased a plot of land on the estate of Count Václav Kounic, the husband of his sister-in-law, Josefina. It was situated at Vysoká, forty miles south of Prague. A single storey house was consequently erected on the foundations of a shepherd's cottage, and there, except during his first visit to America, Dvořák spent a part of every summer.

This enabled him to enjoy the peace of the countryside away from the noisy city, indulging in his favourite hobby, rearing pigeons. Most of his composing was still done in Prague. Vysoká was for relaxation.

The 'Rusalka' villa.

In the following years he concentrated on the works for England: *The Spectre's Bride* (1884), the Seventh Symphony (1884/5), and *St. Ludmilla* (1885/6). In 1887, he wrote the only major choral piece not originally intended for Leeds or Birmingham, the *Mass* in D. Josef Hlávka, an architect and first President of the Czech Academy of Sciences and Arts commissioned it for his private chapel at Lužany. With organ accompaniment, it was performed there on 11 September 1887 with the wives of the composer and Hlávka among the soloists.

The first public hearing took place in Plzeň in the

The view from the garden, looking out towards the small village of Střebsko.

72

One of the many endearing characteristics of Dvořák was his enthusiasm for pigeon-breeding.

following Spring. At the request of Novello & Co., Dvořák orchestrated the *Mass*, and in this version it was presented at Crystal Palace under August Manns on 11 March, 1893. As Simrock was reluctant to accept the work it was published that same year by Novello.

Chapter 9

Dvořák and Tchaikovsky

'My newest but warmest bond of friendship with the great Czech Antonín Dvořák'—Tchaikovsky

In 1887, Tchaikovsky made a successful tour of western Europe conducting his own works. He arrived in Prague in February 1888, meeting Dvořák on 14 February at a concert given in his honour. The two composers became firm friends and, at a dinner given for Tchaikovsky two days later by the 'Russian Circle', Dvořák proposed the toast to the Russian composer. In reply, Tchaikovsky referred to 'my newest but warmest bond of friendship with the great Czech, Antonín Dvořák.'

Dvořák in return presented Tchaikovsky with a signed copy of his Seventh Symphony. On 27 March Tchaikovsky wrote from Vienna to thank him for his kindness:

My dear, good and highly esteemed Friend,
Although it is terribly difficult for me to write in German, I must make use of this Panslav language to tell you that I have often thought of you and that I shall never forget how well and kindly you received me in Prague. Dear Friend, give my kindest regards to Madam, your wife, and allow me to say once more that I am very glad and happy to have won your valued friendship. I hope we may see each other again in November. With a hearty handshake,
I remain, your true friend,
P. Tchaikovsky.

In the following November, Tchaikovsky returned to Prague to conduct his own Fifth Symphony and the Czech première of *Eugene Onegin*. Dvořák wrote to him

Tchaikovsky visited Prague twice in 1888 and conducted two concerts there. The two masters struck up a close friendship.

on 2 January, 1889 expressing his pleasure at hearing the opera:

Dear Friend,

When you were last in Prague, I promised to write to you about your opera *Onegin*. Now not only your request compels me to do so but my inward desire to tell you all that I felt on hearing the work. I confess with pleasure that your opera made a very deep impression upon me, an impression such as I expect from a true work of art, and I do not hesitate to say that none of your compositions has given me as much pleasure as *Onegin*.

It is splendid work, full of warm feeling and poetry, and, at the same time, worked out to the last detail; in short, this music speaks to us and penetrates so deep into our soul that it is unforgettable. Whenever I go to the theatre I feel as if I were in another world.

I congratulate you on this work and pray God you may be spared to give the world many more such compositions.

With a warm embrace
Your devoted
Antonín Dvořák

On 18 January, 1889 from his home in Frolovskoe, Tchaikovsky replied:

75

You cannot imagine how delighted I was with your letter. I value very highly your opinion of my opera not only because you are a great artist but also because you are a man who is frank and sincere. I am exceedingly proud and happy that I have been able to deserve a sincere word of commendation from you, my dear Friend. I thank you once more from the bottom of my heart.

On 13 March Dvořák conducted a concert of his works in Dresden which included the Fifth Symphony the *Nocturne* for strings and the second *Slavonic Rhapsody*. Later the same year, he was awarded the Austrian Order of the Iron Cross, and he and his wife

A letter dated 1889 from Tchaikovsky to Dvořák.

Anton Rubinstein.

had a private audience with the Emperor Franz Josef I.

In March 1890 at the invitation of Tchaikovsky, Dvořák travelled to Russia for a series of concerts. It was now his turn to be honoured with a banquet given by his Russian admirers. On 11 March at the Tsarist Musical Society in Moscow, he conducted the Sixth Symphony, the first *Slavonic Rhapsody*, the *Symphonic Variations* and the adagio from the Serenade in D minor for wind instruments. The *Stabat Mater* was given on 23 March after the composer had left for Petrograd, but not before he had attended the rehearsal. In Petrograd on 22 March the Seventh Symphony and the *Scherzo Capriccioso* were especially well received.

To Gustav Eim in Vienna, Dvořák gave the following account in a letter dated 23 March:

In Petrograd my concert yesterday in the 'Dvorjanskoe

77

The Charles Bridge,
Prague.

sobranie' turned out splendidly for me. The public and the orchestra gave me a very hearty reception and after each movement of the Symphony there was great applause and after the *Capriccio* I had to bow repeatedly. At the Europa Hotel, Rubinstein,[1] President of the Russian Musical Society, gave a banquet in my honour. It was short, but all the heartier. Rubinstein toasted me, Auer,[2] the violinist, drank to the new Doctor of Music (all the papers had a telegram from Prague and so I was pleasantly surprised to learn of it here). I then drank a health to Rubinstein, whereupon the most outstanding musical critic and scholar (they call him the Russian Hanslick), Laroche, toasted me most elegantly and said that the Czechs, though a small nation, stand high in science and art and wished that young Russia would follow our example.

While in Petrograd, Dvořák learnt that the Academic Senate of Charles University in Prague had awarded him the honorary degree of Doctor of Philosophy.

[1] Anton Rubinstein (1829-1894) was a leading composer and Director of the Petrograd Conservatory.
[2] Leopold Auer (1845-1930), the Hungarian violinist, was teaching at the Conservatory.

Chapter 10

Dvořák the Teacher

'And gladly wolde he lerne, and gladly teche'—Chaucer

It was Marie Červinková-Riegrová who was to provide the libretto for Dvořák's next opera, *The Jacobin*. The subject was a tribute to Czech musicians and thereby not likely to have much success abroad.

The Jacobin is set in a Czech town at the time of the French Revolution. Bohus, the Jacobin, the son of a local Count, has been expelled from home for his radical political views. With his wife, Julie, he returns

Maleč Castle home of librettist Marie Červinková-Riegrová (1854-1895).

Marie
Červinková-Riegrová.

in disguise to find his position usurped by his cousin Jiří. He enlists the aid of Benda, the schoolmaster and organist. The character of Benda is modelled on Antonín Liehmann, Dvořák's childhood teacher in Zlonice. It is no coincidence that Benda's daughter is named Terinka, as with Liehmann's daughter.

In the event the librettist grew impatient at Dvořák's long delay (over a year) in starting on the music. The first sketches were made in November, 1887 and the full score completed between March and November, 1888.

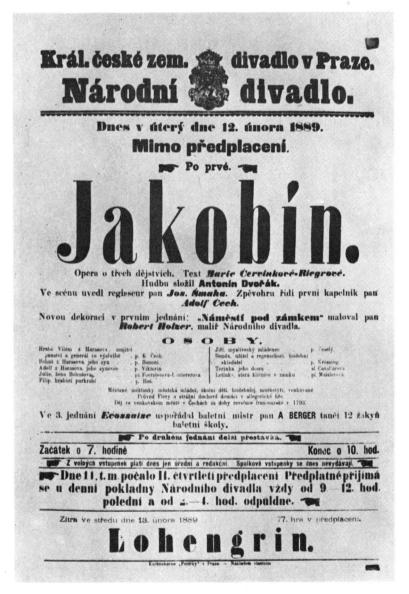

Poster for the first performance of *The Jakobin*.

The Prague
Conservatoire.

Vítězslav Novák
(1870-1949).

The Jacobin was produced at the National Theatre in Prague on 12 February, 1889 under Adolf Čech, and received thirty-four performances in the following five years. As with his other operatic creations, the composer made various alterations after the première and in 1897 he rewrote the second and third acts. Adolf Čech also conducted the revised version at the National Theatre on 19 June, 1898.

In October, 1890 Dvořák joined the staff of the Prague Conservatory as a teacher of composition. The Organ School, Dvořák's *alma mater*, had recently been amalgamated with the Conservatoire. Among his gifted pupils were Josef Suk, who was to marry Dvořák's daughter, Otilie; Oscar Nedbal, later an important conductor and composer of ballets and operettas; Vítězslav Novák, professor of composition at the Prague Conservatory from 1909 to 1939; Rudolf Friml, famous for his many operettas including *Rose Marie, The Vagabond King* and *The Three Musketeers*; and Rudolf Karel, who was to perish in the Terezín concentration camp.

82

Suk and Nedbal were founder members of the Bohemian String Quartet formed by Hanuš Wihan. At the first concert of Dvořák's pupils, on 13 May, 1891, a Piano Quartet by the seventeen-year-old Suk was performed.

As a teacher, Dvořák mixed informality with an insistence on hard work. He made his pupils prepare numerous sketches, making economical use of thematic material. In the funeral oration spoken at Dvořák's grave, Novák said of his master:

What kind of teacher was Dvořák? The answer can only be given in two words: artist–teacher. He was a teacher only for the talented. Pupils who got to him through inadvertence or out of curiosity he managed to get rid of very quickly. 'Music is a liberal art', he would often say on such occasions. He was remarkably practical, submitting each work to a detailed examination, drawing attention to our awkward places and mistakes in very apt comments. 'Sometimes I could howl, but we learnt from it', Josef Suk once sighed. And he was absolutely right. Dvořák's school was strict, but as salutary as a cold douche. Dvořák, however, was never pedantic and praised an original idea with undisguised pleasure.

Another of his pupils, Josef Michl gives an insight into Dvořák's method of improving the work of his students:

The Century Illustrated Monthly Magazine, issue dated July 1894.

Only slowly, often at the cost of bitter experience, did we get to know the Master and grasp his principles and requirements. Unfortunately not even then did we succeed in satisfying our strict Master in every respect. Dvořák had his moods and like every great spirit, he too suffered from so-called 'divine discontent'. So, for example, he would like certain parts in our compositions and on first seeing them he might be positively enthusiastic; later, however, he no longer liked the same parts and required us to change them, improve them or even replace them with better passages. As a result, many compositions or little pieces which were thought to be definitely finished had to be gone over again and sometimes practically recomposed. It can easily be imagined that such work was not as a rule easy, the less so as the Master did not usually indicate how the correction was to be carried out, and he himself only very rarely made the correction. And here we strike on the most typical feature of his method: if he found something (and that happened very often) with which he did not agree and which he wanted to have different and better written, he

Franz Schubert.

forced us to think about it and did not give in until we had
found a better way. It caused us not a few very unpleasant
moments and a lot of difficulty, but to be quite sincere, it
was for us a real blessing. 'What good would it be to you,' he
would say, 'if I were to write it the way it should be! It
wouldn't be yours then and every musician worth his salt
would know that somebody had put it right for you.
Anybody who wants to compose must get accustomed to
think and work independently.'

Dvořák's own wide knowledge of music and
individual concern for each of his pupils is reflected in
Suk's account:

His knowledge of musical works was truly astounding.
Bach, Handel, Gluck, Haydn, Mozart, Beethoven,
Schubert, Berlioz, Wagner, Liszt—he knew the works of all
these masters in detail. He did not dislike Italian music nor
did he share the view of that time that it was 'hurdy-gurdy'

music, and, in general, there was no movement of which he did not take notice; he studied Bruckner, was interested in Richard Strauss and was pleased when he saw among his students a striving towards new and independent expression.

He was interested in everything, nothing in our lives escaped his attention. He liked to read the papers and critical notices, both home and abroad, and regularly read Czech provincial papers, for he took a lively concern in the cultural activities of the country.

Portrait of the composer, 1885.

Central Station, Prague.

Hanuš Wihan, member
of the Czech Quartet.

It is the nature of pupils to venerate their masters especially when they have achieved international fame as composers or performers. But perhaps the best independent testimony we have to Dvořák's remarkable qualities as a teacher is to be found, paradoxically enough, in his own words. We need to abandon a strict chronological sequence at this point and look forward to the year 1894 when, in co-operation with an American scholar Henry T. Finck, Dvořák wrote a lengthy article on Franz Schubert for *The Century Illustrated Monthly Magazine* of New York. Composers are not always at their best when it comes to analysing and commenting upon the works of their peers, but in this article Dvořák reveals his critical as well as his creative genius. Shortly after it was published Sir George Grove—a man not given to unnecessary or to lavish praise—wrote to Dvořák:

I saw your article on Schubert last night, and I lose no time in asking you to accept my best and warmest thanks for it. It is certainly the best and most interesting thing that has ever been written upon that great musician; and every student

Typical locomotives operating through Prague at the height of the Austro-Hungarian Empire.

and every amateur should be grateful to you for thus throwing the light of your genius upon the works and career of your fellow-composer.

I shall read and re-read it until I know it by heart!

The article is reprinted in full as an appendix to John Clapham's authoritative study of Dvořák's music published by Faber and Faber in 1966. In this present volume we must confine ourselves to a few short extracts:

Schubert and Mozart have much in common; in both we find the same delicate sense of instrumental colouring, the same spontaneous and irrepressible flow of melody, the

Josef Suk (1874-1935), Dvořák's son-in-law.

Jeanette Thurber
(1852-1940), founder of
the National
Conservatoire of Music,
New York.

same instinctive command of the means of expression, and
the same versatility in all the branches of their art . . .

Schubert's chamber music, especially his string quartets
and his trios for pianoforte, violin and violoncello, must be
ranked among the very best of their kind in all musical
literature . . .

Of Schubert's symphonies, too, I am such an enthusiastic
admirer that I do not hesitate to place him next to
Beethoven, far above Mendelssohn, as well as above
Schumann . . .

In most of his works Schubert is unique in melody,
rhythm, modulation and orchestration, but from a formal
point of view he is most original in his songs and his short
pieces for the piano . . .

The whole article stands as a model of musical criticism and deserves to be much more widely known. As recently as September 1979, the distinguished pianist Alfred Brendel said* 'I'm terribly excited about it, because there are so many things which are true and commonsense, and quite unusual for that time. He was one of the greatest admirers of Schubert. He gives a lot of insight of a surprisingly modern kind, into the quality of his output.' And, characteristically, Brendel adds a final comment to the effect that this article reveals Dvořák 'as a very nice person too, very sympathetic'.

Dvořák adored trains. Regularly he visited the Franz Josef Station where he noted down the numbers of the locomotives and became personally acquainted with the drivers. On days when he was too busy at the Conservatory, he would send his pupils to the station to take down the numbers of the express trains leaving for European capitals. One anecdote relates that Josef Suk, on such an errand, returned with the numbers of the coal-tenders instead of the engines. In a mock rebuke, the composer said, 'To think that I am letting a man like you marry my daughter!'

The S.S. 'Saale', which took Dvořák on his first visit to America.

* *Records and Recording,* September 1979: interview by Bernard Jacobson.

The members of the
original Czech Quartet
(K. Hoffmann, J. Suk,
O. Berger, O. Nedbal).

In 1891 Dvořák composed the set of three Overtures, *In Nature's Realm, Carnival* and *Othello*, collectively subtitled *Nature, Life and Love*. All three have thematic material in common, but developed in quite different ways to suit the character of the subject. *In Nature's Realm* was dedicated to Cambridge University in gratitude for the degree they had conferred upon him in March of that year. *Carnival* is dedicated to the University of Prague which, in 1890, had granted him a Doctorate in Philosophy.

Othello, the most clearly programmatic of the three, is designed in the form of a symphonic poem, with specific scenes in the play indicated in the score. Although the three overtures were originally intended to be performed as a group, Dvořák instructed his publisher, Simrock, to issue each one individually. They represent one of the composer's highest achievements, and reveal a masterly use of the orchestra.

Prior to his departure for the United States, Dvořák undertook a farewell tour organised by the Prague publisher, Urbánek. Accompanied by Ferdinand Lachner, the violinist and Hanuš Wihan the cellist, they visited, between January and May 1892, thirty-nine towns in Bohemia and Moravia. Their repertoire included the newly composed *Dumky* Trio, the *Mazurek* for violin and piano, and the *Rondo* for cello and piano.

Chapter 11

Dvořák in America

'Wake up, America.'—Augustus P. Gardner

In the spring of 1891, Dvořák received a telegram from Vienna inviting him to be the Director of the New Conservatory of Music in New York. Mrs. Jeanette M. Thurber, the wife of a wealthy New York wholesale grocer had founded this Conservatory in 1885, a project which proved of more lasting value than the operatic ventures she had earlier sponsored, which had cost her and her husband over one and a half million dollars.

She now wanted an international figure in the musical world to add prestige to her institution, asking Adele Margolies, a Viennese pianist teaching in New York to recommend a suitable figure. She in turn consulted her former teacher in Vienna, Anton Door, who suggested either Dvořák or Sibelius.

As Dvořák had failed to reply to an earlier invitation, she sent the following telegram from Paris on 6th June 1891:

Would you accept position Director National Conservatory of Music, New York, October 1892 also lead six concerts of your works?

This proposition, which arrived while Dvořák was in Cambridge, threw the recipient into some confusion. Even after consulting several close friends for advice, he could not make up his mind. To Alois Göbl he wrote:

The directorship of the Conservatoire and to conduct ten concerts of my own compositions for eight months and four

91

New York at the close of the 19th century.

Dvořák's pupil Kovařík (1870-1951) accompanied him on his visit to America.

months vacation, for a yearly salary of 15,000 dollars or over 30,000 gold francs. Should I take it? Or should I not?

After much deliberation, he replied, accepting the concert engagements but declining the directorship. To this Mrs. Thurber was not prepared to agree. The arrival of a draft contract caused the composer to think again. The salary for one year was more than he had received for all his works to date. Even by the standards of today, 15,000 dollars would be a comfortable amount. In 1891 it was a fortune.

With the increasing demands of a large family and doubtless with the promptings of his wife, Dvořák found he could not refuse such a handsome offer. After a few changes in the terms of the contract, and obtaining leave of absence from the Prague Conservatory, he accepted the post for two years.

Mrs. Thurber hoped he would reach the United States in time for the Columbus Fourth Centennial Celebrations on 12 October, 1892. Through Alfred Littleton, who had succeeded his father, Henry, as Director of Novello, she sent Dvořák a copy of Joseph Rodman Drake's poem, *The American Flag,* requesting him to set it for the forthcoming celebrations. As the poem did not reach him until August, Dvořák had already begun to write the *Te Deum,* for soloists, chorus and orchestra for the occasion.

On September 10, he set out from Prague with his wife, his eldest daughter, Otilie, aged fourteen, and his son Antonín, aged nine. They were accompanied by Josef Jan Kovařík, a violinist recently graduated

92

from the Prague Conservatoire, whose father, Josef Kovářík, Snr. had emigrated to the United States where he was choirmaster of St. Wenceslas Church, Spillville, Iowa.

The party sailed from Bremen on 17 September, 1892 in the S.S. Saale. At Southampton, Dvořák sent a telegram to the children who had remained in Prague: 'All is well'. Like Haydn, Dvořák proved a good sailor, remaining on deck during the storms when most of the passengers were languishing in their cabins.

As Kovářík recalled:

The Master proved an excellent sailor; the whole day, it might be as stormy as you like, he walked up and down the deck. Several times it happened that he was the only one to put in an appearance in the dining-room, and when Capt. Rinck saw him alone, he invited him to his table. When they had breakfast or dined at their ease, they lit their cigars and chatted.

They arrived safely in New York on 26 September where they were met by the secretary of the National Conservatory, Mr. Sainton and a group of newsmen who were duly impressed when Dvořák spoke to them

Dvořák's family shortly after their arrival.

in English. One report gives a vivid portrait of the composer.

He is not an awesome personality at all. He is much taller than his pictures would imply, and possesses none of the bulldog ferocity to be encountered in some of them. A man about 5ft. 10 or 11 inches, of great natural dignity, a man of character, Dvořák impresses me as an original, natural and - as Rossini would say - to be natural is greater than to be original.

He is not beautiful in the forms of face, but the lines of his brow are so finely modelled, and there is so much emotional life in the fiery eyes and lined face, that when he lightens up in conversation, his face is not easily forgotten.

The family stayed first at the Clarendon Hotel on East 18th Street, but as they did not care for hotel life, they soon moved to humbler lodgings at 327 East 17th Street, close to the Conservatory.

The National Conservatory of Music was remarkably progressive for the time. It was a non-profit making organisation which offered no diplomas and charged fees only to those who could afford to pay. Dvořák was especially in favour of the policy of giving free tuition to negro students.

His own timetable allowed for three hours of teaching per day and two rehearsals with the orchestra each week. He had a striking influence on his students, encouraging them to evolve a distinctly American music. He told them to search out folk-songs and plantation music for the simplicity of melody free from the heavy domination of European tradition that was stifling originality.

In *Harper's Magazine* of February 1895 he wrote:

These beautiful and varied themes are the product of the soil. They are American. They are the folk-songs of America, and your composers must turn to them. In the negro melodies of America, I discovered all that is needed for a great and noble school of music.

Edward MacDowell, however, one of the first American composers to seek a national character for his music, partly by using American Indian melodies, rejected Dvořák's advice:

We have here in America been offered a pattern for an 'American' national musical costume by the Bohemian,

The Dvořáks took an apartment on East 17th Street soon after they reached new York.

Central Park, where Dvořák took his daily walk.

Carnegie Hall, where the first performance of the *New World* Symphony was given under the baton of Antonin Seidl.

Dvořák—though what negro melodies have to do with Americanism in art remains a mystery. Music that can be made by 'recipe' is not music, but 'tailoring.' Masquerading in the so-called nationalism of negro clothes cut in Bohemia will not help us.

Dvořák developed a particularly close rapport with his negro pupils. Henry Thacker Burleigh introduced him to negro spirituals, and Will Marion Cook later contributed greatly to the early development of jazz.

Other notable students were Rubin Goldmark, later Director of the Juilliard School of Music and teacher of Gershwin and Copland, Harvey Worthington Loomis, an authority on the music of the Red Indians, Harry Rowe Shelley, a composer of much church music, and Edwin Franco Goldman, who developed the concert band repertoire.

James Gibbons Huneker, music critic and essayist, enjoyed many sessions with Dvořák, whom he nicknamed 'Old Borax', when they examined scores and discussed musical matters.

Dvořák's influence affected many composers who were not his pupils at any time. The Violin Sonata and Piano Quintet of Arthur Foote, symphonic works of George Chadwick and the first Symphony of Charles Ives, owe much to the Czech composer in both form and language. The extensive use of folk-songs in 20th Century American music and the 'wide-open-spaces' atmosphere of 'Western' film scores may have at least some of their origins in the orchestral works of Dvořák.

The first concert of Dvořák's music was given in Carnegie Hall on 21 October. The Boston Symphony Orchestra under the composer performed the three Overtures, *In Nature's Realm, Carnival* and *Othello*, and premièred the *Te Deum* with an orchestra of eighty and a choir of three hundred.

Musical life in New York was steadily expanding. The Metropolitan Opera had opened in 1883, and the city boasted two orchestras: the Philharmonic conducted by Anton Seidl and the Symphony Orchestra directed by Walter Damrosch. The noted Kneisel String Quartet from Boston were additionally frequent visitors.

At the end of November, Dvořák travelled to Boston for two performances of the *Requiem*. The orchestra there was directed at this time by the great conductor Arthur Nikisch.

95

Battery Park, from which Dvořák loved to watch the ships in the harbour.

In a letter to Mr. and Mrs. Josef Hlávka, his friends in Prague, Dvořák prophetically recognised the impact that the United States would have on the world in the years that followed.

The first and chief thing is that, thanks be to God, we are all well and liking it here very much. And why shouldn't we when it is so lovely and free here and one can live so much more peacefully—and that is what I need. I do not worry about anything and do my duty and it is all right. There are things here which one must admire and others which I would rather not see, but what can you do, everywhere there is something—, in general, however, it is altogether different here, and if America goes on like this, she will surpass all others.

Madison Square.

Dvořák in 1891.

Although musical education was in its infancy in the United States, Dvořák was optimistic about the potential of the musicians there.

From the same letter he said:

There is more than enough material here and plenty of talent. I have pupils from as far away as San Francisco. They are mostly poor people, but at our Institute teaching is free of charge, anybody who is really talented pays no fees! I have only eight pupils, but some of them are very promising.

And not less so are the entries for the competition for prizes offered by Mrs. Thurber. 1000 dollars for an opera,

1000 dollars for an oratorio, 1000 dollars for a libretto, 500 dollars for a symphony, and 300 dollars each for a cantata, and a concerto.

A great deal of music has come in from all over America and I must go through it all. It does not take much time. I look at the first page and can tell straight away whether it is the work of a dilettante or an artist.

As regards operas, they are very poor and I don't know whether any will be awarded a prize. The other kinds of compositions, such as symphonies, concertos, suites, serenades etc. interest me very much. The composers are all much the same as at home, brought up in the German School, but here and there another spirit, other thoughts, another colouring flashes forth, in short, something Indian (something *à la* Bret Harte). I am very curious how things will develop.

The oratorio prize was awarded to *The Dream King and His Love* by Horatio Parker, a pupil of Rheinberger who was on the staff of the National Conservatory. Henry Schoenfeld won 500 dollars for his *Rural Symphony*.

While in New York, Dvořák was disappointed to find that he could not continue his hobby of visiting the station each day to inspect the locomotives. At Grand Central Station, only *bona fide* passengers were allowed on to the platforms. To overcome this obstacle, Dvořák would travel by overhead tram to 155th Street where he could watch the Chicago and Boston expresses go by.

Josef Kovářík described the composer's new enthusiasm:

The Master found a new hobby in steamships. For one thing the harbour was much nearer and, on the day of departure, the public was allowed on board, an opportunity which the Master made full use of.

There was soon no boat that we had not inspected from stem to stern. The Master always started a conversation with the ship's captain or with his assistants, and so, in a short time, we knew all the captains and mates by name. And when a ship was due to sail we went there and watched it from the shore until it was out of sight. If it happened that the Master remained a little longer than usual at the Conservatory or was engrossed in his work at home and so forgot about the departure of the boat and there was no longer time to go to the harbour, we went by overhead tram to Battery Park and from there following the ship in her outward journey for as long as she remained in sight.

The National Conservatory of Music of America,

126 and 128 East Seventeenth St., New York.

STUDENTS' CONCERT

OF

CHAMBER MUSIC

By DR. DVORAK'S CLASS OF COMPOSITION,

WITH KIND ASSISTANCE OF MR. VICTOR HERBERT,

MONDAY EVENING, MAY 8th, 1893, at Eight o'clock.

PROGRAMME.

SONATA No. 1, C minor, - - HARVEY W. LOOMIS

(PIANO AND VIOLIN)

    a. Allegro Moderato.   *c. Scherzo.*
    b. Romance.   *d. Allegro brioso.*

MR. LOOMIS AND MR. MICHAEL BANNER.

SONGS. - - - LAURA SEDGWICK COLLINS

    a. "Shadowtown."
    b. With Pipe and Flute.

MISS ANNIE WILSON.

"The Boatman." - - - LAURA SEDGWICK COLLINS

CHORUS FOR FEMALE VOICES.

TRIO, D minor, - - - - RUBIN GOLDMARK

    a. Allegro moderato.   *c. Scherzo Vivace.*
    b. Adagio Molto.   *d. Finale, Allegro Confuoco.*

MESSRS. GOLDMARK, BANNER AND HERBERT.

Programme of a concert given by Dvořák's pupils in May, 1893.

In the evening then, after a game of Darda, we discussed with the Master how many knots the ship had probably made where she might be etc. In the morning, the Master's first work was to take the *Herald* and read the shipping news.

With his duties at the Conservatory taking up so much of his energies, Dvořák found less time for composition. In January 1893, he completed *The American Flag*, but its first performance was delayed until 4 May, 1895, shortly after he had finally left the United States. It was published later the same year.

99

Chapter 12

Symphony from the New World

... from all over the hall there are cries of 'Dvořák! Dvořák!' And while the composer is bowing we can see this poet of tone who can move the heart of a great audience.'—New York Herald, 17 December 1893

Soon after arriving in the United States, Dvořák had begun sketching an opera based on Longfellow's *Hiawatha*, a book he had known in a Czech translation for over thirty years. Although nothing came of the project as he could find no suitable libretto, two ideas were incorporated in the Ninth symphony, *From the New World*: the famous cor anglais tune in the slow movement was inspired by the death of Minnehaha, and the scherzo had its origin in an Indian dance.

The first sketches of the Symphony were made in December, 1892, the score being completed in the following May. On the final page he wrote, 'Praise God! Finished on 24 May 1893. The children have arrived at Southampton. Antonín Dvořák. A cable arrived at 1.33 in the afternoon.' In his excitement, he forgot to fill in the closing bars in the trombone parts, an omission not discovered until the first rehearsal.

The principal theme of the first movement was originally conceived in the major, bearing some resemblance to a minstrel song *Little Alabama Coon*, composed by Hattie Starr and sung by Nellie Richards. It was published in 1893 and was widely popular throughout the United States. The cor anglais theme of the slow movement is closely related to another minstrel song, *Massa Dear*.

Except for the C major flute tune in the first

Dvořák's 100th composition whilst in America.

101

The Moravian town of
Kroměříž.

Dr. E. Kozánek.

movement, which some critics consider is derived
from *Swing low, sweet chariot*, and a brief passage on the
violas in the last movement which could have come
from *Yankee Doodle*, there is little that can be easily
identified as 'American'.

The subtitle is *From* the *New World*, and the work
reflects much more a Bohemian looking back to his
homeland. To a friend Dr. Emil Kozánek, a Moravian
from Kroměříž, Dvořák wrote:

I have not much work at school so that I have enough time
for my own work and am now finishing my new symphony
in E minor. I take great pleasure in it and it will differ very
considerably from my others. Well, the *influence* of America
must be felt by everyone who has a *nose* at all.

For the first London performance, Dvořák sent the

102

following information explaining the significance of the title:

I called the symphony 'From the New World' because it was the *very first work* I wrote in America. As to my opinion, I think that the influence of this country (it means the folk songs that are Negro, Indian, Irish, etc.) is to be seen, and that this and all other works written in America differ very much from any earlier works, as much in colour as in character – but I will not criticize myself. I hope that the English people will understand me well, as they did before, and I only regret not being able to be present at the first performance of my work. Will you kindly let me know how the performance turned out or send me some criticism of the London press . . . The Largo goes very slowly as well as the introduction too. Oh, the tempi, the tempi! It is a [*sic*] awful thing!

All the works written in America have one feature in common, melodies comprising one or two-bar phrases repeated in melodic and rhythmical outline. Why this

First page of the manuscript of the *New World* Symphony in E minor.

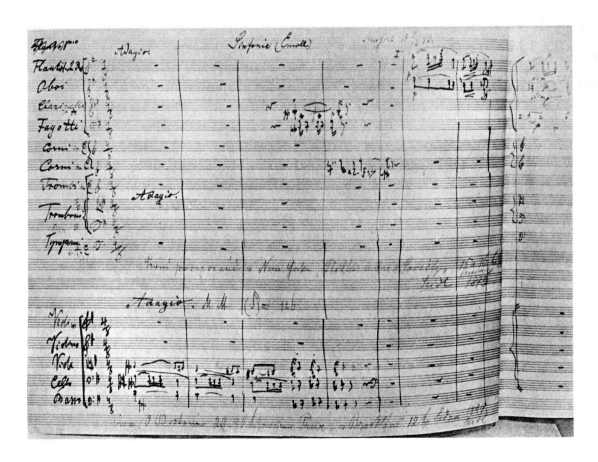

Article in the *New York Herald,* issue dated 16th December, 1893.

is so is hard to explain. The extreme simplicity and repetition of the music of the Red Indians might have exerted some effect upon the composer, but at the time of writing the symphony he had experienced directly very little of their music. Negro spirituals and the songs of Stephen Foster were a source of great interest to him, but short repeated melodic phrases are not a predominating feature of them.

The public rehearsal of the Ninth Symphony at the Carnegie Hall on 15 December 1893, and the première the following day conducted by Anton Seidl were both sensational occasions. The composer received one of the most enthusiastic ovations of his life.

In a letter to Simrock dated 20 December he wrote:

The success of the symphony was tremendous; the papers write that no composer has ever had such a success. I was in a box; the hall was filled with the best New York audience. The people clapped so much that I had to thank them from the box like a king! alla *Mascagni* in Vienna (don't laugh). You know how glad I am if I can avoid such ovations, but there was no getting out of it, and I had to show myself willy-nilly.

Seidl repeated the Symphony on 23 December, and again on 11 January 1894, while on 30 December 1893 Emil Paur conducted the Boston première.

At the suggestion of Kovařík, Dvořák decided not to return to Europe for the vacation. Instead the family travelled to spend the summer at Spillville, a Bohemian settlement in North-East Iowa. Dvořák's sister-in-law, Terezia Koutecká, his wife's eldest sister, brought the other four children from Prague, arriving in New York on 31 May.

On Saturday, 3 June, the Dvořák 'caravan' set off: Dvořák, his wife, their six children, Mrs. Koutecká, a maid and Josef Kovařík. By train they passed through Philadelphia and Pittsburg to Chicago. After a day in Chicago they took another train to Calmar, Iowa. There they were met by Kovařík, Snr., who took them the remaining five miles by carriage.

Dvořák felt completely at home in this community. It reminded him of Vysoká and he was able to take up a similar routine to the one he followed in the summers at home.

In his *Reminiscences*, Kovařík gives a vivid picture of the composer's activities.

Bronze bust by J. Mařatka.

The Master's day in Spillville was more or less as follows: He got up about four in the morning and went for a walk to the river and returned at five. After his walk he worked; at seven he was sitting at the organ in the church. Then he chatted a little, went home, worked again and then went for a walk. He usually went alone—here he had none of the nervous tension from which he sometimes suffered in Prague—and often nobody knew where he had gone. Almost every afternoon he spent in the company of some of the older settlers. He got them to tell him about their bitter and difficult beginnings in America; the old men told him how they went to help with the building of the railway 40 miles from Spillville, and how they went the long way to work on foot, while their wives with the children toiled on the farms.

The streets of Chicago during the World Fair of 1893.

In Spillville the Master scarcely ever talked about music and I think that was one of the reasons he liked being there and why he felt so happy.

In many letters to friends in Czechoslovakia, Dvořák gave detailed accounts of his experiences. To Doctor Kozánek he wrote:

Spillville is a purely Czech settlement, founded by a certain Bavarian, Spielman, who christened the place Spillville. He died four years ago, and in the morning when I go to the church, my way takes me past his grave and strange thoughts always fill my mind at the sight of it as of the graves of many other Czech countrymen who sleep their last sleep here. These people came to this place about forty years ago, mostly from the neighbourhood of Písek, Tábor and Budějovice. All the poorest of the poor, and after great hardships and struggle they are very well off here. I liked to go among the people and they, too, are very fond of me, and especially the grandparents are pleased when I play to them in church 'God before Thy Majesty' and 'A Thousand times we greet Thee'.

106

The peaceful atmosphere of the countryside released a new creative urge. Within two days, 8 to 10 June, he completed sketches for the String Quartet in F, the *American*. The first private performance was given in Spillville with Dvořák as 1st Violin, Kovařík Snr., 2nd Violin, and Kovařík's two children, Cecilia and Josef, playing viola and 'cello. Also dating from this time is the String Quintet in E flat.

For a week during the summer, a group of Kickapoo Indians visited Spillville selling medicinal herbs. They provided song and dance entertainments at the Inn, much to the delight of Dvořák.

On 12 August, the composer travelled to Chicago for the Czech day at the World Exhibition. There, in the Festival Hall, he conducted a concert of his works including the overture *My Home*, three *Slavonic Dances* from Opus 72, and the Eighth Symphony.

The school and the church at Spillville.

On this day there was a great procession of all American Czechs at the Exhibition where a big concert was held and a large Sokol (gymnastic) display. There were about 30,000

The Chicago World Fair,
August 1893.

Czechs in the procession and the concert was in the huge
Festival Hall (orchestra 114 performers) and I conducted my
compositions and Mr. Hlaváč* from Russia conducted the
other works by Czech composers. The orchestra, as also the
performance, was splendid and the enthusiasm general. All
the papers wrote enthusiastically as you will probably read

* Vojtěch I. Hlaváč (1849-1911), a Czech musician who spent most of his life as a
conductor in Russia.

Niagara Falls.

108

The Dvořák monument at Spillville.

Dvořák conducting at the World Fair.

in your papers. The Exhibition is gigantic and to write of it would be a vain undertaking. It must be seen, and seen very often, and still you do not really know anything, there is so much and everything so big truly 'made in America'.

Letter, 17 August 1893, to Antonín Rus.

Dvořák was also honoured with a banquet organised by the Chicago Circle of Czech Musicians.

On a second excursion from Spillville early in September, he travelled to Omaha, Nebraska to see Eduart Rosewater, a wealthy Czech newspaper owner. There also he was treated to a banquet at which there were three hundred guests. Passing through St. Paul, Minnesota, he called on Father Rynda, a Moravian priest whom he had met in Chicago at the World Exhibition. A special banquet was attended by three *thousand* guests.

The highlight of this journey was the Minnehaha Falls. Dvořák noted down on his starched shirt cuff a melody inspired by the sight, which was later used in the slow movement of the Violin Sonatina.

Chapter 13

Return to New York

'The Soul uneasy, and confined from home . . .'–Pope

On 16 September, the family left Spillville to return to New York. At Buffalo, they broke their journey to see Niagara Falls. Its magnificence provoked the comment from the composer, 'My goodness, what a Symphony that would make!'

The second year in New York proved more difficult for the Dvořák family. Mrs Koutecká wrote to Alois Göbl:

In spite of his splendid position and material prosperity he is terribly homesick for his country. Dvořák and Otilie miss home most of all.

The long vacation in Spillville had been a welcome change from the city but it had served as a painful reminder of the joys of Vysoká.

The first public performance of the *American* Quartet was given by the Kneisel Quartet in Boston on New Year's Day, 1894. The same players with an additional viola performed the E flat String Quintet in New York on 12 January. The Sextet in A was also included in the programme.

In January there was a 'Dvořák Evening' given by an excellent quartet from Boston. I sat with my wife among the audience and during the evening I had to rise several times and thank the audience for giving my new works such a splendid reception. All the critics are of the same opinion and one paper, the *New York Daily Herald*, wrote in so many words: 'Why did not Dvořák come to us earlier if he can write such music here in America?'

Letter to Alois Göbl, 27 February, 1894.

During his last year in America, Dvořák composed the *Biblical Songs*, Op. 102 and the Cello Concerto, Op. 104.

In December, 1893 Dvořák composed as a present for his children Otilie and Antonín the delightful *Sonatina* in G for violin and piano. The possible technical limitations of the performers did not inhibit him from producing one of his most spontaneous pieces.

The only other works completed in America before his return to Europe in the summer were the Suite in A for piano, orchestrated the following year, and the set of ten *Biblical Songs*.

The time then came for Dvořák to decide whether to renew his contract at the Conservatory. A serious problem had arisen in Mrs. Thurber's inability to pay Dvořák his full salary, by this time very much overdue. On 28 April, 1894 he signed a contract to return in November for six months on the understanding that he would be paid the 7,500 dollars still owing to him before October.

Three days before sailing on 18 May, he conducted a performance of the *New World* Symphony in New York. Arriving in Prague on 30 May, he went almost at once for a rest to Vysoká.

As autumn approached he grew apprehensive and doubted whether Mrs. Thurber would honour her

111

The Kneisel Quartet in Boston.

agreement to pay the arrears of his salary. On 12 October he cabled to her: 'May be cannot come without receiving all'.

On 9 October she had cabled that half the money had been sent and on 16 October, the composer with his wife and their nine-year old son Otakar, set out for New York. They left Hamburg on the S.S. *Bismark* arriving in New York on 25 October.

To the other five children left in Prague, he wrote:

Otilka (Otilie), you are the oldest and most sensible and I depend on you and also on Anička (Anna). Be good then and, Anynka (Anna), take good care of yourself so that you do not fall ill.

Go,—and remember what I say—often to church; you know, Otilka, what I told you—especially on Sundays see that you go to church. Pray fervently, it is the one thing that can comfort you and us. Look to it that the others, too, Mařka (Magda) and Toník (Antonín), say their prayers. I am not worrying about Zičinka (Aloisie), she will do it all right, the good little soul. More next time. I thank, you, Grandma,

112

for everything, and commend you to God's keeping.
Your loving Father and Mother

The administrative burden at the start of a new year at the Conservatory once more restricted the amount of time that Dvořák could devote to composition. During this final term of office he made revisions to the opera *Dimitrij*, and composed only the Cello Concerto in B minor and the first movement of the String Quartet in A flat. At the same time, the New York Philharmonic Orchestra made him an honorary member and performed the *New World* Symphony and the three Overtures.

Although this second stay in America was much shorter than the first, Dvořák's longing to be back in Czechslovakia was more acute. In a letter to Antonín Rus, dated 18 December, 1894 he revealed how much he missed being with his children:

The children write to us twice a week and we always await the ships coming from Europe expectantly in the hope that they have brought us something. And when a letter does come from the children, you can imagine with what impatience we seize it and read it.

They write that they are well and getting on nicely—only Otla always writes how glad she would be to see us again in Prague. I believe her—and we the same.

With much relief, Dvořák, with his wife and son, left New York on 16 April, 1895 on the S.S. *Saale* which had first taken them to the United States nearly three years earlier. Mrs. Thurber made attempts to entice him back for the next two academic years by sending him draft contracts, but he had no desire to be separated again from his family, his home and his native land, even for a short period of time.

Chapter 14

Back Home

'Happy the wanderer, like Ulysses, who has come happily home at last'—Joachim du Bellay

Upon his return from America, Dvořák enjoyed a few months on holiday, visiting friends and resting at his home in Vysoká. In Karlovy Vary (Carlsbad), he met Hanslick and Simrock.

In her autobiography *When Soft Voices Die*, the pianist Helen Henschel, revealed an appealing side of Dvořák's personality. As a child, on holiday with her mother in Karlovy Vary, she met the composer. With some trepidation she approached him:

'Please may I have your autograph and please would you write a bar of your music for me.' 'Certainly,' said Dvořák. 'What shall I write?' 'Oh please, the slow movement of the *New World* Symphony,' I said, emboldened by the kind smile behind the piercing eyes.

As he took up his pen to write, he suddenly looked at me and mused: 'Let me see, now. I don't think I remember just how it goes. Could you help me?'

My shyness disappeared in my eagerness. 'Oh Yes, Herr Dvořák. It goes like this,' and I proceeded to sing the whole of the first passage. 'Thank you,' he said. 'It begins to come back to me and I think I could write it all if you were to sing it to me once again.' So I did, and it was years before I realised I had been exploited.

In November, 1895 he returned to his teaching post at the Prague Conservatoire. At once he was back in the musical world, visiting Vienna in December and again in the following January. On 16 February, he and Brahms shared a box at the Viennese première of the *New World* Symphony conducted by Richter.

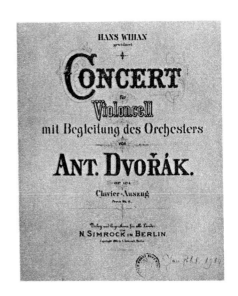

Title page of the manuscript and of the first printed edition of the *Cello Concerto*, Op. 104.

When Brahms played through Dvořák's Cello Concerto with the cellist, Robert Hausmann, Brahms exclaimed:

Had I known that such a cello concerto as that could be written, I would have tried to compose one myself.

Once more, Brahms tried to persuade Dvořák to live in Vienna where he could teach at the Conservatoire. He offered considerable financial assistance to him since the cost of living in the Austrian capital was so high. But the pleasure of returning to Vysoká was too strong for Dvořák to consider living abroad again.

The inspiration of his homeland released a new outpouring of composition. At the end of 1895, he completed his last two String Quartets, the one (begun in America) in A flat, the latter in G.

In the Spring of 1896, he embarked on his final orchestral works. Between January and April he wrote three symphonic poems based once more on Erben's *Bouquet of Folk Tales*. The original stories have particularly gruesome subjects. *The Water Goblin*, for example, tells of a girl who is lured into a lake where she is trapped by a goblin who makes her his wife. When she has a had a child, she returns to her mother. As she fails to go back to the lake, the goblin comes to the house and, after knocking at the door, leaves the headless body of the child on the ground; *The Noonday*

115

Prague from the banks
of the Vltava.

Witch describes the bogy with which mothers threaten their naughty children. When the mother in the poem scolds her child, the witch appears. The horrified mother pleads for her infant, but when the witch flies off, the child is dead.

The story of *The Golden Spinning Wheel*, the most complex of the set, is no less macabre. A young king, out riding, meets a maiden, Dorníčka, who is spinning. On a return visit he tells her step-mother to bring her to the palace so that he can marry her. Instead she kills Dorníčka, cutting off her hands and feet and gouging out her eyes. She goes to the palace, passing off her own daughter as Dorníčka. The king, short of either memory or sight, marries the girl and goes to the wars. An old man finds Dorníčka's corpse and exchanges a golden spinning wheel, a golden distaff and a golden spindle for the missing parts of the girl's body. Dorníčka is restored to life and the spinning wheel in the palace reveals by magic the gory tale. The king puts to death the step-mother and her daughter and marries Dorníčka.

Although all three works were heard at a public rehearsal at the Prague Conservatoire under Antonín Bennewitz on 3 June, 1896, the first concert performances were given in London, *The Golden Spinning Wheel* under Richter, on 26 October, *The Water Goblin* on 14 November and *The Noonday Witch* on 21 November, both conducted by the young Henry J. Wood.

A fourth symphonic poem was composed in October and November of the same year. *The Wild Dove* is also based on an Erben ballad. After she has poisoned her husband, a young widow falls in love with a handsome young man. Following her marriage to him, she is haunted by the cooing of a dove over the grave of her first husband. In despair she drowns herself. None other than Leoš Janáček premièred *The Wild Dove* at Brno, on 20 March, 1897.

A Moravian, himself later to become a highly distinguished composer, Leoš Janáček (1854-1928), had been an ardent admirer of Dvořák's music for many years. In his home town of Brno he conducted the *Slavonic Dances*, the Serenade for Strings, the Fifth and Seventh Symphonies, *The Spectre's Bride* and the *Stabat Mater*. The two men had first met in the 1870's, and in 1883 they went together on a walking tour of

Leoš Janáček.

117

South Bohemia, visiting Dvořák's birthplace at
Nelahozeves.

In the summer of the same year, Janáček stayed in
Dvořák's Prague house while he was away in the
countryside. In 1886, Janáček dedicated his *Songs for
Male Chorus* to Dvořák. In a letter dated 13 September,
Dvořák wrote in answer:

Dear Friend,
   I received your choral works and send you my thanks, not
only for them, but also for the dedication of which I am very
proud and which gives me great pleasure. As soon as I had
opened the parcel, I read them through several times and I
must admit that in many places, especially with regard to

118

your modulations, I was taken aback and unable to form an opinion. I did not go straight away to the piano, I did not play them; I think I understand a thing better, from a theoretical point of view, by merely reading it. But when I had played them through once, twice, three times, my ear gradually became accustomed and I said to myself: well, after all, it may be possible, but we still might argue about it.

That is, however, unimportant. I think they are a real enrichment of our poor literature (poor in that kind of work). They are original, and what is most important they breathe forth a truly Slavonic atmosphere.

Dvořák may well have remembered the time that he, as an unknown composer, had dedicated his D minor String Quartet to Brahms.

Sometime after 1887, Janáček sent Dvořák the score of his first completed opera, *Šárka*, asking for advice. Suggesting certain revisions, Dvořák urged 'more melody, don't be afraid of it.' Although Janáček made extensive changes to the music, the opera was not performed until 1924.

Janáček later expressed his respect in a simple statement:

Do you know how it feels when someone else is taking the words from your mouth? That is how Dvořák has taken his melodies from my heart.

The last of the symphonic poems, *Heroic Song*, has no programme, although the work is thought to represent Dvořák's own artistic destiny. When, in 1898, Mahler succeeded Richter as conductor of the Vienna Philharmonic Orchestra, he wrote to Dvořák on 3 October that year asking if he might give the first performance of the new work. Dvořák attended the première in Vienna on 4 December, 1898. A year later, Mahler introduced *The Wild Dove* to the Austrian capital.

Early in 1897, Dvořák heard that Brahms was seriously ill. In the middle of March he travelled to Vienna to see him. He wrote to Simrock:

Today (19 March), I was in Vienna and visited Herr Brahms and saw how true, unfortunately, is all I heard from you. Nevertheless, let us hope that all is not yet lost. God grant it may be so.

On 2 April, however, Brahms died. Dvořák returned

Gustav Mahler.

119

to Vienna a few days later to be a torch-bearer at the funeral.

Dvořák was appointed to fill the vacancy on the Austrian State Prize Board caused by the death of Brahms. This gave him the greatest satisfaction as he would be able to repay his debt of gratitude for the help he had received when he was poor.

Towards the end of 1898, two events provided the composer with particular personal pleasure. On 17 November, he celebrated his Silver Wedding anniversary, his eldest daughter Otilie at the same time marrying his favourite pupil, Josef Suk. Eight days later, the Emperor Franz Josef conferred upon him the Medal of Honour *pro litteris et artibus*, a distinction given previously to only one other musician: Brahms. Dvořák referred to the huge medal as 'my big gold platter'.

After making revisions to *The Jacobin* in 1897 Dvořák was again searching for a subject for a new opera. The fairy-tale world of the four Erben symphonic poems led him to explore the world of folklore, and the resulting *The Devil and Kate* is based on a story from Božena Němcová's *Fairy Tales* published in 1845. The libretto for this was prepared by Adolf Wenig, nephew of the Director of the Prague National Theatre. The score occupied Dvořák from May 1898 to February 1899. The first performance at the National Theatre on 23 November, 1899 was directed by Adolf Čech. So successful was it, that the opera won an award of 2000 crowns from the Czech Academy of Sciences and Arts.

Kate is an elderly maid who, because of her sharp tongue, cannot find a dancing partner. When she announces that she would dance with Satan himself, Marbuel, a devil from Hell, obligingly appears. After dancing with her, he invites Kate to the underworld and they disappear through a hole in the ground. George, a shepherd, who has been dismissed from the service of the oppressive Lady of the Manor, offers to bring Kate back. Marbuel, a rather timid creature overwhelmed by Kate, wishes her back on earth, and allows George to dance her out of Hell. Marbuel returns to take the Lady of the Manor down to damnation but he is frightened off by Kate.

Chapter 15

Final Years

'Like pilgrims to th' appointed place we tend;
The world's an inn, and death the journey's end.'
—John Dryden

The success of *The Devil and Kate* caused Dvořák to think again of opera. For *Rusalka* he set a text that had been rejected by two of his pupils, Nedbal and Suk. Jaroslav Kvapil (1868-1950) had based his libretto on both the Undine legend and on Hans Andersen's *The Little Mermaid*. As he said:

I received my inspiration in the land of Andersen, on the island of Bornholm, where I was spending my summer holiday. The fairy-tales of Karel Jaromír Erben and Božena Němcová accompanied me to the seashore, and there they merged into one of Andersen's fairy-tales, the love of my childhood days, and the rhythm of Erben's ballads, the most beautiful of Czech ballads.

Rusalka, a water nymph, has fallen in love with a handsome young prince. An old witch grants her wish to become mortal, but on two conditions: that she shall remain dumb, and that if her lover proves unfaithful, she shall return for ever to the lake and he shall die.

When the prince grows tired of the silent nymph, he courts a haughty princess in his castle. Before his eyes, the nymph disappears into a pond. Full of remorse, he seeks her throughout the forest. By the edge of the lake he meets her but at the first embrace, he falls dead and the nymph returns to the water.

The score was begun in April 1900 and completed in November. The first performance–conducted by Karel Kovařovic, who had himself turned down the

(facing page) an excerpt from the actual manuscript score of the opera.

libretto—took place on 31 March, 1901 in the National Theatre. Although Dvořák experienced his greatest theatrical success, it was not performed outside Prague until four years after his death. A projected production in Vienna under Mahler, planned for 1902, was cancelled for contractual reasons.

Rusalka was staged also at Ljublana in 1908 (where it was sung in Slovene), and in Vienna in 1910 by the Brno Opera.

On 14 March, 1901, Dvořák, along with his friend the poet Jaroslav Vrchlický, was elected a member of the Austrian Senate (the *Herrenhaus*). The Prague journalist Josef Penížek recounts one incident:

Each member of the Austrian Senate had in front of him a writing-desk, an inkpot, a sand-sprinkler, blotting paper, several pens and a number of pencils, Hardmut No. 2. soft and yet not brittle, the best product of its kind. Dvořák was delighted with those pencils. He took them all and put them in his pocket. Having left the Senate House, he showed the booty to his wife who was waiting for him and said: 'Look, these will be grand for composing now!'

After the initiation ceremony, Dvořák did not attend the Senate again and his seat there remained empty.

In 1901, Jan Sibelius was taken by Josef Suk (whom he had known in Berlin) to visit Dvořák. The great Finn recalled that:

I was not able to spend much time with Dvořák but it was

Jaroslav Kvapil, librettist of *Rusalka*, and Karel Kovařovic, conductor of the first performance on 31st March 1901.

Dvořák in 1901.

sufficient to give me an extremely favourable impression of him. The old man was naturalness and modesty personified and spoke very modestly of his art, not at all as one would have imagined from his position in the musical life of his country and of the world. Incidentally he said quite sincerely, 'Wissen Sie, ich habe zuviel komponiert (You know, I have composed too much)'. I could not agree with him.

For his last work, the opera *Armida,* Dvořák chose a subject which had been set many times before by other composers including Lully, Handel, Haydn, Gluck and Rossini. The text, by Jaroslav Vrchlický, the poet of *St. Ludmilla* and based on Tasso's *Gerusalemme*

Liberata, had been given to Kovařovic who abandoned the work after completing the first act.

Armida, princess of Damascus, is sent by the Syrian sorcerer, Ismen, into the Christian camp to sow discord and confusion. She captures Tancredi, the Christian champion, who is rescued by Rinaldo. Rinaldo himself is captivated by Armida's magic. When her palace is destroyed, she flies to the Egyptians. She is defeated by Rinaldo, attempts suicide, but is unwittingly killed by Rinaldo.

So different from his nationalistic operas, *Armida* allowed Dvořák to make particular use of the Wagnerian device of *leitmotiv*. The epic nature of the plot was certainly well suited to be treated on Wagnerian lines. The magical element, in particular, recalls *Parsifal* and the heroic postures of the principal characters are similarly Wagnerian in proportion.

The music occupied Dvořák for over a year, from March 1902 to June 1903. He was disappointed that Kovařovic, who had so successfully directed *Rusalka*, declined to conduct the première of *Armida*. The opera was eventually produced at the National Theatre on 25 March, 1904 under Picka.

Reviews were hardly enthusiastic. The cumbersome stage operations and the remote story did not promote the immediate sympathy that had greeted Dvořák's earlier operas, and *Armida* was not performed outside Czechoslovakia until as late as 1961, when it was staged at Bremen.

In August 1903, even before the première of *Armida*, Dvořák had started work on yet another opera, *Horymír* to a libretto by Rudolf Stárel and based on a Czech legend set in the mining district of Březové Hory, near Vysoká. Dvořák's son, Otakar remembered his father's working on the opera:

I have happy memories of the end of the holidays in 1903 when my father had the libretto prepared for the new opera *Horymír* and had even made a number of sketches for it. At Vysoká he told the miners that he was going to write an opera and that in one act there would be real miners and that they would work in a mine with exactly the same machines as they worked with in the mines in the Příbram and Březohorskés. And then father promised them that at the première of the opera the National Theatre must give him the whole auditorium where the miners from Příbram would take their places as the main part of the audience so

Poster advertising the first performance of *Armida*.

The National Museum,
Prague.

Wood engraving by
A. Strnadel.

that they might give their opinion about how far the act
gives the impression of reality. The miners expressed their
doubts as they thought that it would be very difficult to
show a whole mine at the theatre with all its beauties and
terrors. Then father would tell them that all that was the
business of the stage director to see that it was right and
assured the miners that it must be possible when there are
operas where whole acts are played under water or when, as
in one of his operas, a real Hell is conjured up on stage, and
real devils with tails.

126

In an interview given on 1 March, 1904 to the Vienna newspaper, *Die Reichwehr*, Dvořák provided something of *summa summarum* of his views on music at that time:

In the last five years I have written nothing but operas. I wanted to devote all my powers, as long as God gives me the health, to the creation of opera. Not, however, out of any vain desire for glory but because I consider opera the most suitable form for the nation. This music is listened to by the broad masses, whereas when I compose a symphony I might have to wait years for it to be performed. I got a request again from Simrock for chamber works which I keep refusing. My publishers know by now that I shall no longer write anything just for them. They bombard me with questions why I do not compose this or that; these genres have no longer any attraction for me. They look upon me as a composer of symphonies and yet I proved to them long years ago that my main bias is towards dramatic creation.

The Church of St. Salvator in Prague.

Dvořák was still leading a busy life. Later in the same interview he was having to decline invitations to conduct his music throughout Europe:

From the Church of St. Salvator, the funeral procession made its way past the National Theatre and across Dvořák's beloved Charles Square, to the cemetery at Vsyšehrad.

A Requiem was held at the National Theatre in memory of the composer.

Other offers I reject without exception. I got a splendid offer from Berlin. I was to go on a big concert tour with the Berlin Philharmonic Orchestra through Austria, Germany, France and Italy. In London, they offered me the direction of the Popular Concerts of which one concert was to be of my own compositions and I was also to appear as a pianist. Especially as regards the latter, I hesitated very much, because I do not feel so sure of myself as a pianist as to dare to undertake a public appearance. I have also been asked to conduct concerts in Lvov and Warsaw, but I declined all these offers as I do not wish to bind myself.

The end, alas, was nearer than anyone can have expected. It was during the first performance of *Armida* on 25 March, 1904 that Dvořák began to notice the first symptoms of illness. A pain in his side caused him to leave the theatre early. His doctor said it was lumbago, but later he discovered signs of kidney disease.

On March 30th Dvořák caught a chill after visiting the Franz Josef Station to look at his beloved trains. The composer's health had deteriorated sharply, and six days later Professor Hnátek was called in. He immediately diagnosed arteriosclerosis, further complicated by an attack of influenza.

128

Jaroslav Vrchlický (first left), one of the many mourners.

On May Day Dvořák felt well enough to get up, having been confined to his bed the previous ten days. He joined the family for a celebratory lunch, but during the meal complained that he felt unwell. Shortly after, before the doctor had even arrived, he died of a heart attack.

After the funeral on 5 May at the Church of St. Salvator, where the Introit from the *Requiem* was performed, Dvořák's body was taken, amid scenes of great national mourning, to the historic cemetery of Vsyšehrad, where it was laid finally to rest beside the River Vltava.

The grave at Vsyšehrad.

Select Bibliography

Abraham, Gerald. *Slavonic and Romantic Music* (London, 1968).

Clapham, John. *Antonín Dvořák, Musician and Craftsman* (London, 1966).

Clapham, John. *Antonín Dvořák* (London, 1980).

Horějš, Antonín. *Antonín Dvořák, The Composer's Life and Work in Pictures* (Prague, 1955).

Newmarch, Rosa. *The Music of Czechoslovakia* (London, 1942).

Robertson, Alec. *Dvořák* (London, 1945; rev. 1964).

Schönzeler, Hans-Hubert. *Dvořák: His Life and Work.* (London, 1980).

Šourek, Otakar. *Antonín Dvořák, Letters and Reminiscences;* translated by Roberta Finlayson (Prague, 1954).

Šourek, Otakar. *Antonín Dvořák and his Works* (Prague, 1956).

Young, Percy M. *Dvořák* (London, 1970).

Index

Selective list of references
Illustrations are indicated in bold type

133